THE

5

UNANSWERED
QUESTIONS
ABOUT 9/11

THE
5
UNANSWERED
QUESTIONS
ABOUT 9/11

WHAT THE 9/11 COMMISSION
REPORT FAILED TO TELL US

JAMES RIDGEWAY

SEVEN STORIES PRESS

New York | Toronto | London | Melbourne

Seven Stories Press
140 Watts Street
New York, NY 10013
www.sevenstories.com

In Canada: Publishers Group Canada, 250A Carlton Street, Toronto, ON M5A 2L1

In the U.K.: Turnaround Publisher Services Ltd., Unit 3, Olympia Trading Estate, Coburg Road, Wood Green, London N22 6TZ

In Australia: Palgrave Macmillan, 627 Chapel Street, South Yarra, VIC 3141

College professors may order examination copies of Seven Stories Press titles for a free six-month trial period. To order, visit www.sevenstories.com/textbook/ or send a fax on school letterhead to 212-226-1411.

Book design by Jon Gilbert

Library of Congress Cataloging-in-Publication Data
Ridgeway, James, 1936–
   The 5 unanswered questions about 9/11 / James Ridgeway.— 1st Seven Stories Press ed.
      p. cm.
   ISBN-13: 978-1-58322-712-1 (pbk. : alk. paper)
   ISBN-10: 1-58322-712-1 (pbk. : alk. paper)
   1. September 11 Terrorist Attacks, 2001. I. Title: Five unanswered questions about 9/11. II. Title.
HV6432.7.R54 2005
973.931—dc22

                                        2005024128

Printed in Canada

9 8 7 6 5 4 3 2 1

Contents

Acknowledgments

I want to thank David Botti, whose meticulous research made a vital contribution to this book. Natalie Wittlin, George Maurer, and Halley Bondy also provided valuable assistance in research. Special thanks go to Jean Casella, without whose skillful editing this book could never have been completed. I am also grateful to the dedicated staff of Seven Stories Press, and especially its publisher, Dan Simon, for his wise advice and steadfast encouragement.

This book owes a great debt to the whistle-blowers who have braved hostile government reaction and come forward to make public what they know, and who were generous enough to share this knowledge with me. I especially am grateful to Sibel Edmonds, the former FBI translator who not only became a whistle-blower herself, but encouraged others to do likewise. Both Steve Elson and Bogdan Drakovic, former members of the FAA Red Team, have been tireless in their attempts to draw public attention to the failures of that agency, and the resultant risks to public safety. Brian Sullivan in Boston has been a great help. Kyle Hence has provided advice, information, and encouragement from the beginning. Mark Zaid, an attorney versed in national security law, and Allan Duncan, a one man network on the events of 9/11, were also generous with this help. Four years after the attacks, these whistle-blowers, along with the families of the 9/11 victims, have remained unwavering in their demand for responses to all of the unanswered questions about 9/11.

I am also indebted to the many authors whose groundbreaking work helped to inform this book, especially Andrew Thomas's *Aviation Insecurity*, on the air transport industry and its political machinations; Steve Coll's *Ghost Wars*, on the history of the Pakistani secret service in Afghanistan; Senator Bob Graham's *Intelligence Matters*, on failures in the Intelligence Community; and Paul Thompson's *Terror Timeline*, still the most comprehensive summary of events related to the 9/11 attacks.

Preface

How could this have happened?

Of the unanswered questions about 9/11, this is the question that encompasses all others. It is the question most of us asked ourselves while we watched, in shock and near disbelief, as the Twin Towers burned and collapsed on September 11, 2001. It is the question most of us, in one way or another, are still asking.

The 9/11 attacks were events of enormous proportions—enormous in terms of the failure of U.S. institutions as well as the loss of human life. They were events that, for most Americans, produced anger and insecurity as well as sorrow.

One tendency, when faced with such events, is to withdraw into unquestioning patriotism, focusing only on the outside enemy, rather than on homegrown problems. The terrorists are a bunch of evildoers; they hate us for our wonderful way of life and were out to get us; there is nothing we could have done about it.

Another tendency is to grasp at conspiracy theories, envisioning secret, sinister plots reaching to the highest levels of government. Chief among these is the theory that the Bush administration planned or supported the attacks—or, in the less extreme version, that it knew exactly what was going to happen and let the attacks occur because they suited the Bush political agenda. To be fair, there is ample fuel for these theories in the endless cover-ups that have characterized the White House's response to 9/11. But the problem with most of these conspiracy theories (in addition to a lack of convincing evidence to support them) is that they, too, blame what happened on a handful of evildoers; and because they attribute everything to hidden hands, they, too, suggest that there is nothing we could have done about it.

All this misses the point in that it views the fact that 9/11 could happen as something that has to be explained by an aberration—a secret plot, operating outside normal channels. But the circumstances that allowed the attacks to take place, unimpeded, are anything but an aberration. Follow any trail from the events of 9/11 and you come to a point that intersects with the basic structures of the American political and economic system. If this were a conspiracy, then it would have a very large pool of conspirators—all of our captains of business and industry, our scions of political and institutional leadership—and would have been going on for a very long time.

In truth, the hidden hands are hiding in plain sight, and the secret plot is an open secret: Our nation operates on a system designed to serve the interests of those who control money and power, rather than the public interest. We live in a country where other things are simply more important than protecting the lives of ordinary Americans. The fact is that 9/11 happened because other things were more important than making sure it didn't happen.

For example, time and time again, we have seen government regulators place corporate profits before public safety. Should it be any surprise, then, that the FAA allowed airline profits to take precedence over public safety? For decades, the United States has supported unsavory regimes because they served larger foreign policy objectives or possessed vital resources. Does it not follow that we would turn a blind eye to Pakistan's support of the Taliban, or Saudi Arabia's funding of Al Qaeda? The 9/11 Commission

was part of the system, its members drawn from its high eche-
lons. Could we really expect them to produce findings that might
shake the system's foundations?

In saying that "the system" permitted 9/11 to take place, I do
not intend to suggest that what happened was inevitable. Nor do
I think that particular individuals, institutions, or policies should
be held any less responsible for what happened. As this book
shows, there were dozens—perhaps hundreds—of instances in
which a different action, a different choice, or a different priority
might well have prevented the attacks. Especially on the part of
so-called public servants, the choice to serve the system rather
than the public good is an indictment, not a justification.

I also do not mean to take anything away from the culpability
of the Bush administration. There has never, to my mind, been a
White House more intent upon serving corporate interests at the
expense of the public interest—especially when it came to the
interests of the administration's own cronies, from Texas to
Riyadh. The cynical Bush agenda impacted everything from the
regulatory environment to the Intelligence Community, with the
twin priorities of invading Iraq and protecting Bush's friends the
Saudis wiping other vital considerations off the table. Even in the
context of an endemically corrupt system, it reached new depths
in its callous disregard for the welfare of ordinary Americans.
Adding to this were the personal shortcomings of a president who
spent the month before 9/11 cutting timber on his ranch and the
day of 9/11 scuttling from one bunker to another while the vice
president ran the country. America could hardly have been in
worse hands as it faced the devastating attacks.

In fact, my purpose in writing this book and in seeking answers
to these questions is to help readers assign accountability to the
responsible parties—whether they be individuals, agencies, or
long-standing institutions—that failed to protect the 2,800 victims of September 11. The fact that I see no smoking gun—in the

form of a well-defined and purposeful conspiracy to support or per-
mit the attacks—doesn't mean that no crime has taken place.
Negligence, after all, can be criminal. And sometimes it can be
impossible to see a smoking gun, because the air is already so thick
with smoke.

1

Why Couldn't We Stop an Attack from the Skies?

HOW THE AIRLINES AND THE FAA RESISTED AIR SECURITY
MEASURES THAT MIGHT HAVE SAVED LIVES

At 7:02 in the evening of December 21, 1988, Pan Am Flight
103, a Boeing 747 on its way from London to New York,
exploded 31,000 feet above the village of Lockerbie, Scotland,
killing all 259 people on board and eleven on the ground. The
bomb on board, later attributed to Libyan terrorists, consisted of
an electronic timer attached to plastic explosives and hidden in a
Toshiba cassette player. The cassette player had been placed inside
a brown Samsonite suitcase labeled with stolen luggage tags. The
unaccompanied suitcase was then put aboard an Air Malta flight
from Malta to Frankfurt, where it was transferred to Pan Am's
Frankfurt-London-New York flight.

While the bombing of Pan Am 103 was hardly the first incident of terrorism aboard a commercial airplane, it significantly
increased public awareness of air terror. The public response to devastating media images of remains scattered over the quiet Scottish
countryside, along with the persistent demands for answers by
the victims' families, forced both the airline industry and the U.S.
government to take a serious look at air security.

Yet nearly thirteen years later, on September 11, 2001, the

world was watching another devastating series of media images: not only the sight of commercial airliners being flown into the World Trade Center, but also the surveillance camera footage of the hijackers walking casually through the security checkpoints at Boston's Logan Airport on their way to board the planes.

The attacks demonstrated an utter lack of effective air security in the United States, where more than 518 million people travel on more than 9 million commercial flights every year. This disaster was a long time coming, and the warning signs were everywhere. But even the loudest warnings were not heeded.

How could this have happened? This question has yet to be adequately answered by the airlines or by the Federal Aviation Administration, which regulates and oversees the industry. Clearly, the airline industry, like all corporate entities, is driven by profits and thus resistant to implementing security measures that would cost them money. But unlike most corporate entities, this particular industry holds the lives of millions in its hands. It was the job of the government, through the FAA, to ensure that these lives were protected. The FAA proved itself grossly unworthy to hold that responsibility.

It is difficult to say which is more horrifying: the knowledge that the attacks might have been prevented if the FAA had done its job, or the knowledge that—with no one held accountable and few real changes made—it could all happen again tomorrow.

WHO REGULATES THE REGULATORS?

Most of the federal government's regulatory agencies were set up during the New Deal to provide a measure of public scrutiny to the nation's basic industries. In more recent times, they have often been criticized as inefficient, ineffective, and not sufficiently independent from the industries they are meant to regulate.

For example, the federal government's one effort to regulate the petroleum came when the Federal Power Commission made a halfhearted attempt to control the price of natural gas during the 1960s; the industry fought it tooth and nail, and the government soon gave up any effort to regulate energy. The Federal Trade Commission made only feeble gestures toward employing the antitrust laws in the interests of achieving auto safety. The Interstate Communications Commission has never been able to withstand the pressures of big broadcasting. And the Federal Aviation Administration, charged with overseeing the airlines, is candidly viewed in Washington as a captive of that industry.

Corporate resistance to government regulation made considerable strides during the deregulation boom that began not under Ronald Reagan, but under Jimmy Carter, with support from liberal Democrats. It was Carter who initiated the process of deregulating natural gas in the late 1970s, following the energy crisis. Senator Ted Kennedy unexpectedly joined the deregulation lobby with a proposal to deregulate the airline industry, abolishing the Civil Aeronautics Board and ending strict rules on airline schedules and prices. Kennedy reportedly introduced the bill on the advice of an aide, Stephen Breyer—then a Senate committee staffer, later appointed to the Supreme Court by President Clinton. Breyer, one of the architects of "pollution credits," has promoted the idea that industries function best when they are released from supposed government strangulation and exposed to the refreshing breezes of the free market.[1] By the time Ronald Reagan came to power in 1980s, the deregulation trend had already been well established, and he was all too happy to see it taken to the next level.

Deregulation helped free the hands of the airline companies, allowing them to organize their business with reduced government oversight and interference. This included limiting mandates for security measures—especially when those measures might adversely affect the airlines' bottom line. It also included blunting the teeth of the federal agency responsible for regulating airline safety, the

FAA, which operates as part of the Department of Transportation. In his book *Aviation Insecurity*, Andrew Thomas writes, "In short, market forces ran rampant through the agency for decades and eventually marginalized the FAA and its security functions."[2]

The commercial airline companies have paid well for their freedom from government scrutiny. In the year 2000 alone, the air transport industry spent $46 million on lobbyists.[3] Airlines have long blanketed Washington with a coterie of well-heeled and influential lobbyists, many with friends in high places. As Thomas documents, William Coleman, former secretary of transportation in the Ford administration, has been a lobbyist for US Airways. George Mitchell, another influential figure in Washington politics with long-standing ties to the Democratic leadership in Congress and the Clinton White House, became a lobbyist for Northwest Airlines after he retired from the Senate in 1995. Former Oregon senator Bob Packwood lobbied for United Airlines, as did Harold Ickes, Clinton's deputy chief of staff.[4]

Linda Daschle, wife of Senator and former Democratic Senate Majority Leader Tom Daschle, is considered one of the most powerful airline industry lobbyists in Washington. Doug Ireland, writing in the *LA Weekly*, documented Daschle's history as an industry shill. She lobbied for the Air Transport Association, the industry's main trade association, beginning in the 1980s. She then became the senior vice president of the American Association of Airport Executives. In yet another turn of the revolving door between government and industry, Daschle became FAA deputy administrator under Clinton from 1993 to 1997. For the last few months of her tenure there she was acting administrator, the top job at FAA; during this brief period, she vigorously opposed criminal background checks for airport employees, echoing the position of the airlines. Daschle then joined a top lobbying firm, where her largest client was American Airlines (others included Northwest Airlines and Boeing).[5]

Even before the 9/11 hijackings of two American Airlines planes, Linda Daschle had her work cut out for her. American had previously been involved in six fatal crashes.[6] It had been fined millions of dollars for breaking safety rules and was widely viewed as the most unsafe of the major carriers. Among other things, Daschle fought against regulations that would have required reinforced cockpit doors and costly security measures at airport checkpoints—measures that might have prevented the 9/11 hijackings.[7]

The airline companies also have a history of giving handsomely to both political parties during elections. According to a report by the Center for Responsive Politics, total contributions by the air transport industry for the 2003–4 election cycle came to $13.1 million. Airlines, a subgroup within the industry, gave $2.7 million, two-thirds of it going to Republican candidates. AMR Corp., the parent company of American Airlines, was among the top five contributors, with donations of $549,666, of which 63 percent went to Republicans.[8]

To backstop its powerful lobby, the airlines exercise control over FAA advisory committees—which are supposed to provide public input into rule making and policy, but are, in fact, heavily dominated by industry. In *Aviation Insecurity*, Thomas gives as an example an aviation security advisory committee from 2000: of nine nongovernmental members, six represented airlines and airports, leaving just three other seats—one for airline employees, one for local law enforcement, and one for the passengers.[9]

WHY DIDN'T PAST AIR DISASTERS CHANGE THINGS AT THE FAA?

Even all of the lobbying resources of the airlines could not completely quiet public demands for action in response to high-profile incidents like airplane bombings or hijackings. The FAA had to at least go through the motions of addressing the security failures in these cases.

The United States first took a closer look at how civilian aviation was protecting itself against hijackings following a series of incidents in the 1960s and 1970s where Cuban refugees seeking to return home seized airplanes. In retrospect, these seem pretty tame affairs. There never was any attempt to harm passengers or crew and certainly nothing aimed at bringing down governments. (More than twenty years later, the 9/11 Commission would conclude that the FAA's response protocols were still geared toward this type of hijacking.[10])

Following the Cuban hijackings, Congress provided FAA with laws and enforcement authority to protect American aviation from future hijackings. One section of the FAA, Flight Standards, concerned itself with air-rage incidents, and the other, the FAA's Security Division, concentrated on airport and ground security. Its mission statement said the purpose of FAA Security was to prevent security incidents and to "protect the flying public." But from the start, many risks to the "flying public" were swept under the rug, while others were duly noted in various official reports and recommendations, but never acted upon.[11]

In 1988 the FAA did a security assessment of the Frankfurt airport, one of the largest air-travel hubs in Europe. The report concluded, "Security at Frankfurt is held together by tenuous threads of luck."[12] The FAA took no action. It was in December of that year that Pan Am Flight 103 blew up over Scotland. The unaccompanied suitcase that held the bomb had been loaded onto the plane from a connecting flight at Frankfurt Airport, Pan Am 103's point of origin.

The United States' initial response to the Pan Am 103 bombing seemed almost routine. The FAA sent a team to investigate. It took seven months of intense pressuring by the victims' families before President George H.W. Bush, in the *Washington Post*'s words, "reluctantly formed" a commission on August 4, 1989. The president's Commission on Aviation Security and Terrorism made a host of findings and recommendations, thirty-one of them directed at the FAA. Even after some of these recommendations were reinforced by the Civil Aviation Act of 1990, most were implemented halfheartedly, ineffectively, or not at all.[13]

For example, Congress proposed ten-year criminal background checks on all employees at the nation's airports. (There were suspicions that airline employees might have helped smuggle the bomb onto Flight 103.) The industry promptly opposed this idea, claiming it would add to the airlines' administrative costs. They also said it would end up irritating travelers, since the airlines planned to pass on heightened security costs by raising ticket prices. To fight the proposed changes the industry hired William Webster, former head of both the CIA and FBI. In the end, existing airport employees were exempted from the new law, making it essentially toothless.[14]

A similar scenario followed the July 17, 1996, crash of TWA Flight 800. Shortly after taking off from New York's JFK airport, the Boeing 747, which was headed for Paris, exploded over the Atlantic south of Long Island, instantly killing all 230 aboard. The ostensible cause was a spark in the plane's fuel tank, although several eyewitnesses reported seeing the plane hit by something that looked like a missile, and theories varied from terrorism to a military exercise gone wrong.

In any case, shortly after the crash President Clinton appointed the White House Commission on Aviation Safety and Security, headed by Vice President Al Gore, to examine security within the industry—and especially security against possible terrorist attacks.

Writing in the *Boston Globe* shortly after the 9/11 attacks, Walter Robinson and Glen Johnson retraced what had happened when the Gore Commission made its findings public. A preliminary report, released in September 1996, elicited a flurry of unhappy responses from airline lobbyists. Gore quickly capitulated to the airline industry, writing a sheepish letter to Carol Hallet, president of the Air Transport Association, the industry trade group: "I want to make it very clear that it is not the intent of this administration or of the Commission to create a hardship for the air transportation industry"; he also suggested that government and industry could work "in full partnership." According to a study conducted by the Center for Responsive Politics, during the final weeks of the 1996 election campaign, with Clinton pitted against Bob Dole, the airlines poured $585,000 into the Democratic party coffers.[15]

The Gore Commission did make some fifty recommendations, but many of the most vital proposals were gutted or simply ignored. The Commission again recommended criminal background checks for airport security personnel, along with a changed work system that would reward good performance rather than just low costs in assessing both the individual security staff and the security companies used by the airlines. The airlines scoffed that these measures would be too expensive, and the FAA (then under the leadership of Linda Daschle) never pursued them.

One Commission member, Victoria Cummock, widow of a Pan Am 103 victim, wrote to Gore, "I register my dissent with the final report. . . . Sadly, the overall emphasis of the recommendations reflects a clear commitment to the enhancement of aviation at the expense of the Commission's mandate of enhancing aviation safety and security. I can not sign a report that blatantly allows the American flying public to be regularly placed at unnecessary risk."[16] Cummock was quoted by CNN as saying, "I don't know how we could really get a fair commission based on the degree of collusion that I see between the [airline] industry, the FAA, the DOT [Department of Transportation], and Al Gore."[17] In a suit against Gore and the Department of Transportation, Cummock alleged "that the Vice-President forced her to abandon a call for specific counter-terrorism measures and demands for their implementation."[18]

Terrorism in the air took on new dimensions with the discovery, in the mid-1990s, of the so-called Bojinka Plot in the Philippines. This involved an Al Qaeda scheme to blow up a dozen American airliners in a single operation by putting bombs on board. The plotters set up a jury-rigged laboratory in a Philippines apartment, where they came up with a design for a bomb that could pass through screening devices. All it required was a Casio watch, a bottle of what looked like contact lens solution but was actually nitroglycerin, and a couple of tiny batteries. These were to be packed separately and then quickly assembled into a lethal explosive on board the airplane. The scheme was ingenious because the bomber would get aboard the plane in the Philippines, build and place the bomb, then depart at the first stopover. All of this would take place outside the United States, and no visas were required. After the planes took off again, the alarm would go off on the watch and the bomb would explode.

To test their handiwork, the group put a bomb under a seat in a Manila movie theater, and then, on December 1, 1994, hid one in the life jacket stowed beneath a seat on a Philippine Airlines flight out of Manila bound for Tokyo. Al Qaeda member Ramzi Yousuf—who had also been connected to the first World Trade Center bombing—got off the plane at Cebu, a Philippine resort spot, and the bomb went off on the second leg of the flight, ripping through the fuselage and killing the Japanese businessman who was in the seat directly above it. Ten other people were hurt, but the plane was able to make an emergency landing in Okinawa.

The main plot to blow up twelve American airliners with thousands of passengers was averted by chance. In a makeshift explosives laboratory in a Manila apartment, chemicals mixed and started a fire. Hastily departing operatives left behind a laptop computer containing crucial documents, including a list of the planes to be bombed.

One of the men connected with the plot, Abdul Murad, was subsequently arrested and interrogated in the Philippines; in addition to the plot to blow up a dozen planes, Murad spoke of plans for using hijacked planes as missiles in suicide attacks on the Pentagon and CIA headquarters.

Abdul Murad had also attended two flight schools in the United States, and by 1996, the FBI had begun investigating flight schools where suspected Middle Eastern terrorists might be training.[19] Here were two clear indicators of the methods that would be used on 9/11, five years or more before the attacks.

WHY WAS THE "RED TEAM" IGNORED?

One potentially useful response to the rising incidence of air terror had been implemented following the Pan Am 103 crash. The FAA had been directed by Congress to create a "Red Team" to test airport security. A Red Team consists of a handful of people, often drawn from military special operations, who pose as terrorists and attempt to break through airport security—staging, in effect, unannounced mock terrorist attacks and reporting on the airlines' performance in thwarting these attacks. Two former members of the FAA Red Team have turned whistle-blowers, speaking frankly about their experiences during the 1990s: Steve Elson, a former Navy SEAL, joined the team in 1992. Bogdan Dzakovic, a former field agent and air marshal, joined in 1995.[20]

The team reported to the FAA's Assistant Administrator for Civil Aviation Security, a position created by the 1990 Civil Aviation Security Act. The first person to hold this position was retired Marine general O. K. Steele. According to Bogdan Dzakovic, Steele was particularly effective in raising standards for air marshals, who had been known to nap in airplane lavatories and leave their guns behind when they got up from their seats. During Steele's three-year term, the new Red Team instituted a new kind of security test. Up to that point, the FAA, in conjunction with the airlines, ran tests that showed an above 90 percent success rate by airports in their efforts to block terrorists. After the Red Team used real time simulation exercises, the success rates turned into 90 percent failure rates.

Despite this new evidence, and in the absence of any actual new terrorist disasters, there was little enthusiasm at the FAA or elsewhere for an active response—especially if it would cost money. As Steele would testify to the 9/11 Commission, by the time he left his position in 1993, "There had been no serious mishaps or breaches into the 'system' and thus security was once again taking a back seat to other more pressing concerns. Even my own agency had earlier cut the 120 new ACS positions that had been planned for that year. Moreover, the depressed state that the airline industry was in had stiffened their resistance to making new security investments."[21]

It was up to Steele's successor, Cathal Flynn, to push the aviation security program forward. Flynn was a rear admiral with a thirty-year career in the Navy. But Flynn was viewed by many as overly cooperative with the airlines. It was during Flynn's long tenure as Associate Administrator for Civil Aviation Security (1993–2000) that a slew of information emerged about commercial airplanes' vulnerability to terrorism. But these years were marked by an almost complete lack of action in response to heightened awareness of threats to aviation security.

As early as 1992, an FAA internal intelligence report documented incidents of terrorism aboard civilian airliners over the previous decade, stating, "Small knives (blade length of four inches or less), the most frequently employed weapon to hijack aircraft (in the US), were used in three incidents." The report then discusses overseas incidents and air terrorism in general, concluding, "It should not be presupposed from this, however, that such hijackings will never occur in the US. Politically-motivated hijackings by multiple hijackers have, in fact, taken place in the US, but not within the past nine years."[22]

Much testing was carried out under the direction of the Department of Transportation's Office of the Inspector General (OIG). With more than four hundred employees, the OIG was charged with providing "programmatic oversight and guidance" to all sectors of the DOT, from cost controls to highway safety to airport security. Mary Schiavo, who became Inspector General in 1990, developed a reputation for being aggressive about safety violations. Much of her work focused on lax mechanical inspections, faulty airplane parts, and overburdened air traffic control systems, but she also drew attention to airport security.

A 1993 draft report from Schiavo's Office of the Inspector General portrays airport security as being in dismal shape and concludes, "it is reasonable to believe that these findings could be symptomatic of a much larger problem." (The airports covered in the audit were BWI, Miami, San Francisco, San Juan, and Houston Intercontinental.) This 1993 report shows that three out of five times, people without authorization made it through the San Francisco airport security system—a 60 percent failure rate.[23]

But too often, when testing yielded unpalatable results, these results were buried—and testing was stopped altogether. A May 21, 1996, letter from the FAA security chief Cathal Flynn to Karl-Heinz Hemmer, a senior German aviation official at Frankfurt airport, discusses the results of the Red Team's testing program to see whether the airport and airlines had corrected the sloppy baggage screening that allowed the bomb to be smuggled aboard Pan Am 103. Out of thirteen tries to get past security screening at Frankfurt, the Red Team succeeded all thirteen times, for a 100 percent failure rate. Cathal Flynn, according to his own letter, "elected to inform the U.S. carriers in Frankfurt of these results to see whether detection performance would improve." But even after this tip-off from the FAA, it was, as Flynn wrote, "clear that the results have not changed. Accordingly, I have decided now to conclude the project with our current total of 31 assessments," rather than the sixty that had been planned.[24] This sudden halt to testing, according to Bogdan Dzakovic, was typical of the FAA's security operations during the Flynn years. When the results of the Red Team's testing looked too negative, the Team was simply called off, and follow-up testing was cancelled.

The following month, in June 1996, Congressional hearings were held after a Valujet plane crashed in the Florida Everglades. The cause was a fire in the cargo bay—not terrorism—but the FAA failed to take action on the discount airline's abysmal safety record, and Inspector General Mary Schiavo took the opportunity to speak of the "culture of unaccountability" at the FAA and mentioned that it was nicknamed "the tombstone agency" because it acted only after a deadly air disaster—in other words, it took dead passengers to make the FAA do anything.[25] Schiavo quit the agency the following month. (She is now an attorney representing families of air disaster victims—including some from 9/11.)

In 1997 the FAA conducted another round of secret tests of airport security to try and isolate weak points. This testing was supposed to be kept secret from airport managers, and the airlines and field agents were threatened with discipline and even firing if they told anyone. But one testing subcontractor found out what was going on and told an FAA field office in Michigan. That led to a memo issued by Bruce Butterworth, then working under Cathal Flynn as head of security operations. "Indeed, we did tell the [airline] Industry when the tests would start and how long they would last, and something generally about their coverage. We also, of course, briefed them on what deficiencies we found last time. Before anyone jumps to a conclusion, let me assure you: No, this is not the way we will be operating."[26] In fact, it turned out to be exactly the way the FAA was operating, time and time again.

In 1998, Red Team member Bogdan Dzakovic dropped in unannounced to check out the San Juan airport and found a gaping hole in that airport's security. When cruise ships returned to San Juan, they would haul all the passengers and baggage to the airport and dump them. In a report, Dzakovic wrote that in these cases, the airport's "current infrastructure was so overwhelmed with passengers that the air carrier simply stopped conducting certain basic security requirements during the peak travel times." Dzakovic was ordered to remove this passage from his report, and the program of unannounced inspections was ended. Nothing changed in San Juan.[27]

Frustrated by the numerous instances in which the Red Team's warnings went unheeded, Dzakovic wrote a memo on August 14, 1998, to FAA administrator Jane Garvey. Going over the heads of his immediate supervisors, Dzakovic set forth the numerous failings of the airport security system, pleading with Garvey to act before people got needlessly killed. "The US faces a potential tidal wave of terrorists attacks," he wrote. Garvey never acknowledged getting the memo. When Dzakovic went to Secretary of Transportation Rodney Slater, Slater directed Garvey to reply—but the reply never came.[28]

An October 1998 internal memo from one airline describes a meeting held the previous month with the FAA to discuss security at the San Francisco airport. Among other things, the report noted that the FAA's Red Team "worked around different areas in SFO airport. They managed to break through different security screenings repeatedly in many different areas. Of 450 times when they were working their way past different security points to get to secure areas they were caught only 4 times." San Francisco was one of the airports that had been targeted in the 1993 tests and

cited for a 60 percent failure rate. Five years later, the failure rate
was 99.11 percent.

The report stated that the Red Team "managed to get by passenger X-ray screening repeatedly (seven times) having on them
a gun sealed under their belt-buckle. Also, having an automatic
Mac machine gun under their jacket on their back." The team
also easily entered the airlines' private lounges and put bombs in
the passengers' carry-on luggage, which was not examined before
they boarded the plane. Gaining entrance to the ramp area, they
entered Skychef catering trucks and with ease placed whatever
they wanted in the food trolleys. No one questioned them. "Most
of the times the catering truck driver was either asleep or reading
a book or just looking at the sky or waving a friendly hello,"
according to the San Fransisco report. The intruders showed false
IDs and then easily drove a van onto the ramp area, although the
vehicle had no official plates or security seals. They boarded aircraft at will and "could easily have placed a bomb on board."

All of this activity was videotaped by the Naval Surface Warfare Center at Port Hueneme, California, with the idea of using
it as a training film for airport security personnel. But when the
FAA saw how bad things were, they deep-sixed the video.[29]

When airline security violations could not be ignored or buried
altogether, they were rendered inconsequential to the airlines' bottom line. For example, when the FAA levied fines against the airlines (already a concession, since the agency might have pursued
harsher measures), they were routinely negotiated down in special
administrative hearings, sometimes to as little as ten cents on the
dollar. In 1999, the three largest U.S. airlines were each cited for
more than five hundred violations; but the fines, clearly, had simply become part of the cost of doing business and still cheaper
than implementing better security practices.[30]

Repeatedly, in the late 1990s, efforts to run unannounced
inspections at major airports were thwarted by the FAA higher-ups,

who tipped off the airports before the undercover inspectors arrived. At the same time, no actions were taken to correct problems identified in the past. Year after year, the same measures were discussed and rediscussed—and never implemented. For example, says former Red Team member Steve Elson, "When I came to FAA in 1992, I found out that, as early as 1990, some in FAA Security had been recommending hardening and locking of the cockpit doors. No action was taken to effect these recommendations."[31]

This was despite ample evidence of how easily cockpits could be breached. As Andrew Thomas reports in *Aviation Insecurity*, in the two years prior to September 11, 2001, passengers managed to enter the cockpits of commercial airplanes thirty times. In one 2000 case, a passenger aboard a Southwest Airlines flight was suffocated to death—apparently by other passengers—after he made repeated attempts to take over the cockpit. In another case the same year, a deranged passenger entered the cockpit of a British Airways 747, bit the captain's ear, grabbed the controls, shut off the autopilot, and sent the plane into a ten-thousand-foot dive before the copilot managed to regain control. Lack of cockpit security would, of course, become key to the terrorists' success in the 9/11 attacks.[32]

Both Red Team whistle-blowers made repeated attempts to get higher-ups to act upon their findings. Steve Elson finally quit the FAA in frustration in February 1999. He then launched a personal effort to change the agency policy. He visited the office of FAA administrator Jane Garvey, with no success. He then turned to the Office of the Inspector General, now headed by Schiavo's replacement, Kenneth Mead (who remains in place today). In May 1999, Elson met with Todd Zinser, chief criminal investigator for the OIG, and took the following notes:

> Discussed FAA failures, cover-ups, and the abysmal state of AVSEC [aviation security]. As

proof, I related the events that occurred during my change of planes en route to Washington. In approximately five minutes, I had obtained jetway door combinations; opened, but did not breach a jetway door; obtained serialized bag tags; and picked up a set of "stray" keys which gave me access to restricted documents and restricted areas in the airport. When Mr. Zinser asked for those items, I gave them to him, obtaining a dated receipt. During the course of our discussions (while driving south on I-395 past the Pentagon), he stated, "The whole FAA is so corrupt I don't know where to begin."

Bogdan Dzakovic also spoke with Todd Zinser, who told him that to be able to take action against the FAA, since the departure of Mary Schiavo, would require "a smoking gun in the hand of the shooter standing over the dead body."[33]

This "culture of compromise," as Andrew Thomas calls it, affected the attitudes of agency personnel. In a 2000 employee attitude survey of FAA security specialists, 56 percent said that they did not trust agency management, and only 10 percent said they did.[34]

In addition to the warnings from whistle-blowers from inside the FAA, shortcomings in civil aviation security were resoundingly documented by the Government Accounting Office (GAO). Buried in a note in the *9/11 Commission Report* is a long list of GAO reports on the subject: "Aviation Security: Additional Actions Needed to Meet Domestic and International Challenges" (January 27, 1994), "Aviation Security: Urgent Issues Need to Be Addressed" (September 11, 1996), "Aviation Security: Slow Progress in Addressing Long-Standing Screener Performance Problems" (March 16, 2000)—and the list goes on.[35]

Yet when he testified before the 9/11 Commission, Cathal Flynn, who remained head of Civil Aviation Security until December 2000, spoke of the agency's success at addressing security concerns:

> The FAA conducted an increasingly well-focused and intensive program of tests, assessments, and audits to measure the performance of all elements of the security program, to ensure compliance, and support enforcement actions. The results were consolidated, analyzed, and presented to regulated entities. . . . By 2000, the national security baseline had been raised as intended. Its baseline effectiveness was adequate for the conditions of low threat that prevailed. It could be made more stringent when heightened threats required it. There was an active, continuing program to identify specific weaknesses and fix them, and to improve the entire program over time. It was adequate to fill its role in national anti-terrorism strategy. In order to defeat the defenses at airports and around airliners, terrorists would need to organize, plan, prepare, and rehearse their attacks in ways that would come to the attention of the national intelligence community.[36]

In precisely the time period Flynn describes, the 9/11 hijackers were beginning to "organize, plan, prepare, and rehearse their attacks," and no one at all seemed to notice. Mohammed Atta is known to have spent time closely observing security at Boston's Logan Airport, from which two of the four hijacked planes would take off. According to Andrew Thomas, "For years, Logan was known throughout the industry as one of the least secure airports in the nation."[37]

In April 2001, Deborah Sherman of Boston's Fox 5 station undertook her own investigation of air security at Logan Airport, with the help of former Red Team member Steve Elson. Airing on May 6, 2001, her report showed serious security flaws, including knives smuggled through security and unguarded access to secure areas—making Logan clearly vulnerable to terrorist attack.[38]

The report had been instigated by Brian Sullivan, an FAA New England security agent who had retired earlier in the year and was seeking to blow the whistle on what he had observed on the job. On May 7, the day after the program aired, Sullivan sent a tape, along with a detailed and eloquent letter, to Senator John Kerry: "This report once again demonstrated what every FAA line agent already knows, the airport passenger screening system simply doesn't work as intended. The FAA would like [to] continue to promulgate a façade of security, than to honestly assess the system. Management knows how ineffective the current system is, but continues to tell Congress that our airport screening is an effective deterrent."

Sullivan's letter argued that the FAA was still working with a 1970s model when it came to hijacking: "Do you see a horde of Cuban exiles just waiting to commit air piracy to return to Havana? Or has the threat become more refined over the years?" He expressed his fear of what might happen if aviation security failed to evolve to respond to new threats: "With the concept of jihad, do you think it would be difficult for a determined terrorist to get on a plane and destroy himself and all other passengers? . . . Think what the result would be of a coordinated attack which took down several domestic flights on the same day. The problem is that with our current screening system, this is more than possible. Given time, with current threats, it is almost likely."[39]

Sullivan received no response from Kerry, and the senator's

office did not respond to calls from reporter Deborah Sherman. After 9/11, Kerry told a Fox 5 reporter in Washington that he had sent the tape to the Department of Transportation but did not know what they had done with it. Kerry declared that the "FAA should be held accountable"—but he had taken no steps to ensure their accountability, even for their conduct in his own state.[40]

Rank-and-file security agents like Brian Sullivan joined the Red Team members and other whistle-blowers in pressing for action in response to increasingly alarming reports of wide-open security breaches in the system run by the airlines under the supervision of the FAA. They turned not only to top FAA officials, but also to Congress—where they received expressions of concern, but still no action. Even when they turned to the media, there were rumblings and gestures—but still no significant action. The reason was clear, as it had always been: The FAA's primary concern was to support the industry it was supposed to regulate, even at the expense of public safety in a time of growing threats.

This attitude is evident in a memo sent by Michael Canavan, who took Cathal Flynn's place as Associate Administrator for Civil Aviation Security, to high-level security managers. Although Canavan (who quit his job after 9/11) was widely considered to be tougher on the airlines than his predecessor, his letter nonetheless reflects the long-standing culture of compromise that characterized the FAA's relationship with the airlines. The letter is dated May 30, 2001, less than three and a half months before the 9/11 attacks. In it, he emphasizes the "philosophy" that is to guide FAA responses to security breaches by the airlines:

> The safety and security of the flying public will depend upon the FAA and industry maintaining a candid, respectful, and mutually responsive business relationship. To be effective in this relationship, we need to be flexible. . . . [T]here will

be times when we find areas of noncompliance. When we do, I want to fully consider the actions the party has taken to fix the problem. I want to work with industry to develop action plans to permanently correct problems. . . . To encourage industry to join us in this effort I do not expect us to impose a civil penalty against a regulated party for certain unaggravated violations. . . . I want to give our partners a realistic opportunity to comply with the regulations and to work with us.[41]

While the FAA was working with its "partners," the airlines, to "develop action plans," the 9/11 hijackers were putting the finishing touches on their own actions plans.

WHAT DID THE FAA KNOW AND WHEN DID THEY KNOW IT?

The final, published report of the 9/11 Commission studiously avoids finger-pointing in general. But it seems especially restrained when it comes to accountability at the FAA. When the 9/11 Commission questioned FAA officials like Jane Garvey and Cathal Flynn in 2003, their questions were, for the most part, softballs. Most commissioners seemed to accept the idea that the FAA, like the military, simply did not expect the kind of plane-as-missile suicide attacks that took place on 9/11. The *9/11 Commission Report* reviews the FAA and the North American Aerospace Defense Command's (NORAD) existing protocols for dealing with hijackings and concludes, "On the morning of 9/11, the existing protocol was unsuited in every respect for what was about to happen."[42]

The Commission concluded that the FAA had done the best they could in a difficult situation that they could not have anticipated.

"The details of what happened on the morning of September 11 are complex, but they play out a simple theme. NORAD and the FAA were unprepared for the type of attacks launched against the United States on September 11, 2001. They struggled, under difficult circumstances, to improvise a homeland defense against an unprecedented challenge they had never before encountered and had never trained to meet."[43]

It may well be true that on-the-ground FAA personnel in local command centers, like most of NORAD's military personnel, had no inkling that these kinds of attacks might be possible. But the same was not true of high-level FAA intelligence and security officials—as the 9/11 Commission has long known, even if the public has not.

A staff report completed by the Commission in August 2004, but not partially declassified until February 2005, went further than the published report in holding the FAA responsible for its lack of preparation on 9/11: "The fact that the civil aviation system seems to have been lulled into a false sense of security is striking not only because of what happened on 9/11 but also in light of the intelligence assessments, including those conducted by the F.A.A.'s own security branch, that raised alarms about the growing terrorist threat to civil aviation throughout the 1990's and into the new century," the report said.[44]

As the *New York Times* summarized it on the day following its release, "The report takes the F.A.A. to task for failing to pursue domestic security measures that could conceivably have altered the events of Sept. 11, 2001, like toughening airport screening procedures for weapons or expanding the use of on-flight air marshals. The report . . . said officials appeared more concerned with reducing airline congestion, lessening delays, and easing airlines' financial woes than deterring a terrorist attack."[45] In particular, the staff report reveals just how much the FAA knew in the months leading up to September 11, 2001. "The FAA had indeed considered the possibility that terrorists would hijack a plane and use it as a weapon. In the spring of 2001, FAA intelligence distributed an unclassified CD-ROM presentation to air carriers and airports, including Logan, Newark and Dulles, the three sources of the hijacked planes. The presentation cited the possibility that terrorists might conduct suicide hijackings but stated, fortunately we have no indication that any group is currently thinking in that direction."[46]

The staff report cites other evidence of the FAA's suspicions: "Between March 14 and May 15, 2001, the FAA's Office of Civil Aviation Intelligence conducted a series of classified briefings for security officials at 19 of the nation's largest airports, including Newark, Boston's Logan and Washington Dulles. The briefing highlighted the threat posed by terrorists in general and Bin Ladin in particular, including his threats against aviation. The renewed interest in hijacking by terrorist groups was also covered." An FAA liaison to the intelligence community told the Commission that U.S. intelligence thought "something was going to happen" in the summer—but probably abroad. Despite their focus on hijackings overseas, the FAA warned airports that if "the intent of the hijacker is not to exchange hostages for prisoners, but to commit suicide in a spectacular explosion, a domestic hijacking would probably be preferable."[47]

The FAA's claims that it thought hijacking was only a problem overseas is also belied by a change proposed to its regulations on July 17, 2001, in which "the FAA expressly cited the presence of terrorist cells in the United States and their interest in targeting the transportation sector."[48]

In the six months prior to 9/11, FAA senior officials received fifty-two intelligence briefings regarding threats from Al Qaeda. "Among the 105 summaries issued between April 1, 2001 and September 10, 2001, almost half mentioned Bin Ladin, Al Qaeda, or both, mostly in regard to overseas threats," the report said. In addition, the National Security Council's Counterterrorism Security Group invited the FAA to a "meeting in early July 2001 at the White House to discuss with domestic agency officials heightened security concerns."[49]

The FAA also sent out informational circulars to warn airports and air carriers about security issues. Seven circulars were sent before 9/11—one on the threat posed by surface-to-air missiles, five on threats overseas, and one on July 31 mentioning hijacking. Yet while Jane Garvey said "she was aware of the heightened threat during the summer of 2001," several other top agency officials as well as senior airline official and veteran pilots said they were not aware of it.[50]

The history of the staff report itself is almost as damning as the history it describes. As the *New York Times* reported, "The Bush administration has blocked the public release of the full, classified version of the report for more than five months, officials said, much to the frustration of former commission members who say it provides a critical understanding of the failures of the civil aviation system. The administration provided both the classified report and a declassified, 120-page version to the National Archives two weeks ago and, even with heavy redactions in some areas, the declassified version provides the firmest evidence to date about the warnings that aviation officials received concerning the threat of an attack on airliners and the failure to take steps to deter it."[51] 9/11 Commission chair Thomas Kean criticized the five-month delay in the report's release. "There is nothing in the report which adversely affects national security, but some of the things redacted might prove embarrassing to the FAA."[52]

It might also have proved embarrassing, of course, to President Bush, on whose watch all of this had taken place. Had the report been released five months earlier, it would have become public before the presidential election. It would, in fact, have appeared in the days leading up to the Republican National Convention, where Bush was promoting himself as the man who could keep America safe from terrorists. The ultimate release of the report even followed, by two weeks, the confirmation as secretary of state of Condoleeza Rice, the woman who had been assigned primary responsibility for national security on 9/11, and who had assured the Commission that any warnings of Al Qaeda's intent to attack within the United States was "historical information based on old reporting." (See chapter 3.)

WHAT HAPPENED IN THE SKIES ON 9/11?

What happened on 9/11, aboard the four doomed flights, reveals many things. It demonstrates the utter lack of preparedness on the part of the FAA to respond to such an attack. It shows the terrible consequences of decades of inadequate regulation of commercial aviation by the FAA. It exposes the incompetence—and in one case, the near criminal treachery—of the airline companies themselves in dealing with a crisis. And it highlights the courage of a handful of flight personnel and passengers, who deserve to be counted among the heroes of 9/11.

An enormous amount of the responsibility for dealing with these or any hijacked planes clearly rested with the FAA. It was the job of the FAA's regional control centers to notify higher-ups at the FAA of any suspected hijacking. Control centers relevant during 9/11 were located in Boston, New York, Indianapolis, and Cleveland. This notification, according to protocol, would swiftly reach the FAA command center in Herndon, Virginia, as well as FAA headquarters in Washington. The head of the Office of Civil Aviation Security was supposed to be the hijack coordinator for the FAA. It was the hijack coordinator's job to get in touch with the National Military Command Center, which would obtain authorization for military actions from the secretary of defense. The FAA would then assist and collaborate with NORAD, providing them with information about plane locations, communications from pilots and crew, and the like.[53]

The private airline companies also had their responsibilities and operated under clearly defined protocols for hijackings. The Air Carrier Standard Security Program required that airlines immediately contact both the FAA and the FBI in the event of a suspected hijacking.[54]

The airlines were also supposed to screen the passengers and baggage going aboard their planes with sufficient rigor to keep the flying public safe, while the FAA was supposed to set adequate security standards and see that they were met.

Almost none of these imperatives, of course, were met on 9/11.

To begin with, all nineteen of the 9/11 hijackers passed through airport security checkpoints run by private security companies, which had long been held to low performance standards by airlines that claimed they lacked the money to demand better. Several of the hijackers were flagged for special security measures, which simply meant that their bags were not loaded onto the planes until they themselves were aboard. One was questioned because he did not have a photo I.D.; his bags, too, were held back. At least two of the hijackers set off metal detectors; they were cursorily "wanded" and allowed to proceed. As the *9/11 Report* puts it, "By 8:00 a.m., . . . they had defeated all the security layers that America's civil aviation system had in place to prevent a hijacking."[55]

AMERICAN AIRLINES FLIGHT 11 took off from Boston's Logan Airport at 7:59 a.m. At 8:13 it stopped responding to instructions from Boston air traffic controllers, and some time in the next few minutes, its transponder—the device that provides a plane's location and altitude to controllers—was shut off. According to some accounts, at that point, Boston controllers already considered the flight a "possible hijacking." But they contacted no one.[56]

Then began a series of remarkable communications from two coach class flight attendants on Flight 11, Betty Ong and Madeline "Amy" Sweeney. Within five or six minutes of the hijacking, Betty Ong made a call to an American Airlines reservations agent and was eventually patched in to a supervisor, Nydia Gonzalez. Gonzalez also called a manager at the American Airlines operations center in Fort Worth, Texas, and, with a phone to each ear, relayed what Ong was saying.

Ong's call was recorded, and four and a half minutes (with one "momentary blank") were replayed at the 9/11 Commission hearings. A portion of the recording follows:

> BETTY ONG: We're . . . just left Boston, we're up in the air.
>
> FEMALE VOICE: I know, what . . .
>
> BETTY ONG: We're supposed to go to LA, and the cockpit's not answering their phone.
>
> FEMALE VOICE: Okay, but what seat are you sitting in? What's the number of your seat?
>
> BETTY ONG: Okay, I'm in my jump seat right now.
>
> FEMALE VOICE: Okay.
>
> BETTY ONG: At 3R.
>
> FEMALE VOICE: Okay.
>
> MALE VOICE: Okay, you're the flight attendant? I'm sorry, did you say you're the flight attendant?
>
> BETTY ONG: Hello?
>
> FEMALE VOICE: Yes, hello.
>
> MALE VOICE: What is your name?
>
> BETTY ONG: Hi, you're going to have to speak up, I can't hear you.

MALE VOICE: Sure. What is your name?

BETTY ONG: Okay, my name is Betty Ong. I'm number 3 on Flight 11.

MALE VOICE: Okay.

BETTY ONG: And the cockpit is not answering their phone. And there's somebody stabbed in business class. And there's . . . we can't breathe in business class. Somebody's got mace or something.

MALE VOICE: Can you describe the person that you said—someone is what in business class?

BETTY ONG: I'm sitting in the back. Somebody's coming back from business. If you can hold on for one second, they're coming back . . .

BETTY ONG: Okay. Our number 1 got stabbed. Our purser is stabbed. Nobody knows who stabbed who, and we can't even get up to business class right now cause nobody can breathe. Our number 1 is stabbed right now. And who else is . . .

MALE VOICE: Okay, and do we . . .

BETTY ONG: And our number 5—our first-class passengers are—galley flight attendant and our purser has been stabbed. And we can't get into the cockpit, the door won't open. Hello?

MALE VOICE: Yeah, I'm taking it down. All the information. We're also, you know, of course, recording this. At this point . . .

FEMALE VOICE: This is Operations. What flight number are we talking about?

MALE VOICE: Flight 12.

FEMALE VOICE: Flight 12? Okay. I'm getting . . .

BETTY ONG: No. We're on Flight 11 right now. This is Flight 11.

MALE VOICE: It's Flight 11, I'm sorry, Nydia.

BETTY ONG: Boston to Los Angeles.

MALE VOICE: Yes.

BETTY ONG: Our number 1 has been stabbed and our 5 has been stabbed. Can anybody get up to the cockpit? Can anybody get up to the cockpit? Okay. We can't even get into the cockpit. We don't know who's up there.

MALE VOICE: Well, if they were shrewd they would keep the door closed and—

BETTY ONG: I'm sorry?

MALE VOICE: Would they not maintain a sterile cockpit?

BETTY ONG: I think the guys are up there. They might have gone there — jammed their way up there or something. Nobody can call the cockpit. We can't even get inside. Is anybody still there?

MALE VOICE: Yes, we're still here.

FEMALE VOICE: Okay.

BETTY ONG: I'm staying on the line as well.

MALE VOICE: Okay.

NYDIA GONZALEZ: Hi, who is calling reservations? Is this one of the flight attendants, or who? Who are you, hun?

MALE VOICE: She gave her name as Betty Ong.

BETTY ONG: Yeah, I'm number 3. I'm number 3 on this flight—and we're the first . . .

NYDIA GONZALEZ: You're number 3 on this
flight?
BETTY ONG: Yes and I have. . .
NYDIA GONZALEZ: And this is Flight 11? From
where to where?
BETTY ONG: Flight 11.
NYDIA GONZALEZ: Have you guys called any-
one else?
BETTY ONG: No. Somebody's calling medical
and we can't get a doc—[57]

Ong acted calmly under intense pressure, desperately trying
to provide vital information about the hijacking. But she was
interrogated by ground personnel who seem skeptical about her
story. (Apparently, other portions of the tape have them saying it
might be air rage, rather than a hijacking.[58]) Ong was forced to
repeat the same basic details again and again. Still, she remained
on the phone for twenty-three minutes, calmly relaying information up to seconds before the moment of impact, when the call
ended with the words, "Pray for us. Pray for us."[59]

Flight attendant Amy Sweeney also began telephoning to the
ground shortly after the hijacking. According to the *9/11 Commission Report*, Sweeney made two calls to the American Airlines
flight services office at Logan. She was cut off twice, and time was
wasted while American Airlines personnel, who mistakenly
thought Sweeney was on Flight 12, tried to investigate a plane
that had not yet taken off. But by 8:32, Sweeney reached the
office's supervisor, Michael Woodward.[60]

According to Woodward, Amy Sweeney began speaking to
him, calmly and in a low voice: "Listen to me, listen to me very
carefully." Woodward was a friend, so he immediately believed
what she was saying and began to take notes. She proceeded to tell
him that a hijacking was underway and described the storming of

the cockpit. She said that the first-class flight attendants had been stabbed, a passenger had had his throat slit, and the hijackers had brought something that looked like a bomb into the cockpit.

Woodward dialed out on another phone and began relaying what Sweeney was telling him to the supervisor of pursers at Logan, who simultaneously transmitted it to American Airlines headquarters in Fort Worth. Sweeney provided Woodward with the seat numbers of the hijackers. He had a colleague look up the passengers' names and relayed these to another American official.[61] Woodward remained on the phone with Sweeney until minutes before the crash. Many of the passengers in coach did not fully understand what was going on. But Sweeney, who did, looked out the window as the plane lost altitude over New York City and told Woodward that she could see water and buildings.[62] "We are flying very, very low," she said. "Oh my God, we are way too low." Then the call ended.[63]

In June 2004, family members of the victims on the four 9/11 flights attended a briefing in Princeton, New Jersey, arranged by the FBI. There, they heard a tape, which had reportedly "just surfaced," of conversations among managers on duty at American Airlines headquarters when information began coming in from the two flight attendants. Family members were forbidden to disclose what they heard (because, they were told, it was part of the case the FBI was building against accused 9/11 conspirator Zacarias Moussaoui), but several of them became so outraged by the tape that they broke the gag order. According to Gail Sheehy's account in the *New York Observer*, family members reported that the American Airlines tape reveals an immediate concern for secrecy, with such statements as, "Don't spread this around. Keep it close"; "Keep it quiet"; and "Let's keep this among ourselves. What else can we find out from our own sources about what's going on?" According to a former American Airlines employee who heard the tape, two managers in Systems

Operations Control were saying to one another, "Do not pass this along. Let's keep it right here."[64]

Because of the presence of mind of these two flight attendants, American Airlines' top officials in Fort Worth knew, within moments of the event, that one of their planes had been hijacked. They knew that the hijackers had stabbed and probably killed their own employees, as well as passengers. And because both Ong and Sweeney provided seat numbers, they had an idea who the hijackers were. By 8:30, details from Ong's account had reached American Airlines Executive Vice President Gerard Arpey, who was effectively in charge of the company that morning.[65] There is no record that American Airlines called the FAA's central Command Center, other local control centers, the FBI, the military, or their own pilots, in the air or on the ground. According to the *9/11 Report*, an air traffic control specialist at American Airlines did contact the Boston control center about ten minutes after they first learned of Ong's call, but by that time Boston was already well aware of the hijacking.[66]

At the Boston control center, controllers had watched Flight 11 veer even farther off course. Then, at 8:24, through the cockpit's talk-back button, which had been activated, they heard the hijackers say, "We have some planes," and warn passengers to stay quiet and not move. The Boston flight controllers initially followed FAA protocol, relaying news of a confirmed hijack to some other regional control centers, and then, at 8:28, to the FAA Command Center in Herndon, Virginia. The Operations Center at FAA headquarters in Washington was also notified. A conference call was established among various centers, and top FAA officials were made aware of what was going on. But no one in FAA leadership followed the clearly designated procedure for such incidents, which is to contact NORAD.

Eventually, the Boston control center attempted to directly contact nearby Otis Air National Guard Base and then an Atlantic

City, New Jersey, air base, which had been taken off alert status years earlier due to budget cuts. NORAD's northeast headquarters (NEADS) was not notified until at least 8:37—thirteen minutes after the hijackers had been heard in the cockpit, and about twenty minutes after the transponder signal was lost and Betty Ong made her call to report the hijacking.[67]

The military response was hindered by a shortage of accurate information about locations and by the absence of clear rules of engagement. It was also hindered by a lack of time. By the time fighters from Otis Air Force Base were in the air and headed for New York, the World Trade Center was in flames.

To date, most discussions of the delayed responses by the airlines and the FAA have questioned whether the military might have had time to stop Flight 11 if they had known of the hijacking sooner. This seems possible, though not likely. What seems far, far more likely is that rapid and by-the-book reactions from the airlines and the FAA might well have prevented the hijackings on at least one of the other planes and possibly all three. Considering what was at stake, relatively little investigative work or public discussion has focused on this question.

Another little-explored issue concerns reports of a gun aboard Flight 11. An initial FAA executive summary of the events of 9/11, apparently sent to Jane Garvey at 5:30 that afternoon, stated that one passenger on the plane was shot, not stabbed to death. The memo said that this information had come from the operations center at American Airlines corporate headquarters and was based on conversations with a flight attendant. It was quite detailed, including the time of the single shot (9:20), the name of the hijacker who fired the gun, and the name and seat number of the passenger who was killed (identified by an Israeli newspaper as a former member of a secret Israeli counterterrorist unit).[68] The FAA called the memo, which had been leaked, a "first draft," but declined to release the final draft of the memo because it was "protected information." American Airlines denied the existence of a gun or gunfire aboard Flight 11. The presence of a gun would, of course, represent a far more serious breach of airport security and potentially increase the airline's liability.

UNITED AIRLINES FLIGHT 175 was the second plane to take off, leaving Logan at 8:14 a.m. At 8:42, the pilots reported to ground control in New York that they had heard a suspicious transmission from another plane: "It sounded like someone keyed the mikes and said, 'Everyone stay in your seats.'" The plane was hijacked moments later; its transponder signal changed at 8:47. This was more than twenty minutes after Flight 11 had been confirmed as a hijack and seconds after it had crashed into the Twin Towers—but the pilots and crew on Flight 175 had no way of knowing this.

At about 8:51, a New York flight controller began to recognize the signs of a hijacking aboard Flight 175 and managed to warn a nearby plane that it was on a collision course with the hijacked plane; it missed Flight 175 by 200 feet. Flight 175, already off course, made a U-turn and headed for New York. It did not respond to the controller's attempts to contact the cockpit. A few minutes later, news of a possible hijack was reported to a manager, who tried to alert regional managers but was told they could not be disturbed because they were discussing a hijacking (Flight 11).[69]

At "about 8:50," United Airlines' operations center outside Chicago received the news that controllers had lost contact with Flight 175, and an unidentified flight attendant had called United's maintenance center in San Francisco to report that "the crew has been killed, a flight attendant has been stabbed. We've been hijacked." There is no evidence that United notified either the FAA's Command Center or NORAD.[70]

Phone calls from those aboard Flight 175 to relatives on the ground suggest that passengers had a fuller awareness of what was happening and had begun to discuss trying to storm the cockpit just moments before the plane hit the second World Trade Center tower at 9:03.[71]

The FAA Command Center had only a few minutes' notice of the hijacking before the plane crashed; New York finally notified them at 9:01. They did not pass this information on to NORAD, which learned of the hijacking from New York just as the plane was hitting the tower.[72]

Those with vital information about both of the first two hijackings failed to pass this information on to those who most needed to know. In addition to keeping the information from the military, no one, apparently, thought to inform anyone who occupied potential targets—the landmarks, or even the cities, toward which the planes were aimed.

It is important to remember that all four of the planes hijacked on 9/11 were transcontinental flights. To head for their intended targets, they had to veer far off course—in some cases, making complete U-turns. Flight 11 turned toward New York about twenty minutes before it hit the World Trade Center. With Flight 175, the trajectory toward New York was less clear, but the head of the New York control center said he knew where it was headed at least ten minutes before the crash. In both cases, the hijackings were confirmed even earlier in the timeline.

On the ground, workers in the World Trade Center, along with New York City Mayor Rudolph Giuliani, other local officials, and uniformed services had no warning about Flight 11. Worse still, even after Flight 11 hit the North Tower, they believed it was an accident. And they made decisions based on this knowledge, even as a second hijacked plane was speeding toward New York, targeting the South Tower. In the South Tower, at about 8:50, tenants were informed via the public address system that the incident was limited to the other tower, that their building was safe, and that they should remain in or return to their offices. These instructions apparently came from the World

Trade Center's own fire safety personnel (who died in the building's collapse). Some companies and many individuals chose to leave anyway. But many stayed in the building—and some even headed back upstairs, to floors that would be destroyed by the crash. At 8:57, official word came from the New York City Fire Department to evacuate the South Tower, because of general concerns about structural safety. The order to "begin an orderly evacuation" was passed on to tenants on the PA system at 9:02, less than a minute before impact. Seventeen minutes passed between the first crash and the second.

As the 9/11 Commission notes, "Clearly, the prospect of a second plane hitting the second tower was beyond the contemplation of anyone giving advice. According to one of the first fire chiefs to arrive, such a scenario was unimaginable, 'beyond our consciousness.'"[73]

Would this scenario have been "unimaginable" had the fire chiefs—or anyone else on the ground in New York—known that the first crash was not an accident, but an intentional act of terrorism, using a hijacked plane as a missile to destroy a famous landmark and kill ordinary civilians? Would it have been "beyond their consciousness" if they had known that a second plane had also been hijacked?

The evacuation of the Twin Towers, once it began in earnest, took place with amazing speed. Had local officials known about the hijackings, it is likely that they would have ordered immediate and rapid evacuations. In the South Tower, especially, many of the tenants in the impact zones, and some of those who worked above and were cut off from escape routes, might have had time to get to lower floors before the plane hit and then exit the building safely before it collapsed. But they had lacked the information they needed to make decisions that might have saved their lives. They literally did not know what was hitting them.

AMERICAN AIRLINES FLIGHT 77 left Dulles airport at 8:20 a.m. At 8:54, it veered off course and two minutes later its transponder was shut off and it disappeared from the radar of the Indianapolis control center, which was then monitoring the flight. The hijacking of Flight 77 apparently did not take place until half an hour after American Airlines headquarters had first learned of the hijacking of Flight 11. By 8:45, American had sent pages to its top executives and management personnel alerting them to a confirmed hijack. It had also activated its own emergency command center, where managers gathered to watch the radar blip of Flight 11 until it disappeared over New York City.[74] But it didn't tell its pilots.

Shortly before 9:00, after learning that Flight 77 was missing and believed hijacked, American's Executive Vice President Gerard Arpey instructed other American Airlines flights in the northeast not to take off. United followed soon after.[75] But still, American did not notify their pilots in the air.

When Flight 77 disappeared from radar, controllers in Indianapolis thought it must have crashed due to mechanical failure. By 9:08, they had even contacted Air Force Search and Rescue and the West Virginia State Police and asked them to look for a downed plane. The reason for their misapprehension was simple: no one had informed the Indianapolis control center that any planes had been hijacked that morning, even though two planes had already hit the World Trade Center.

Indianapolis finally learned of the hijackings at 9:20 and realized what was probably happening on Flight 77. But because they thought the plane had crashed—and because of errors and technical glitches with the radar—Indianapolis controllers did not realize that the plane had turned around and headed outside their airspace. Not until 9:32, after the FAA Command Center notified other centers to look for the plane, did Dulles controllers locate Flight 77 on its radar. As the 9/11 Commission reported, "Although the Command Center learned Flight 77 was missing, neither it nor FAA headquarters issued an all points bulletin to surrounding centers to look for primary radar targets. American 77 traveled undetected for 36 minutes, on a course heading due east for Washington, D.C."[76]

The flight path of Flight 77 gave an especially clear indication of its intended target city. Because it took off from Dulles, outside Washington, traveling west, it had to make a complete U-turn after it was hijacked in order to head back toward its target. The plane flew straight toward the Washington area for more than thirty minutes—adequate time to evacuate potential targets in Washington, which are all low-rise buildings. Surely the Pentagon would have been counted among these targets. But no one in the Pentagon—or in the Capitol or the White House—knew that the plane was coming.

The military had no opportunity to respond to the hijacking of Flight 77. Instead, in the minutes before Flight 77 crashed, NORAD was trying to sort out erroneous information, received from the FAA, which said that Flight 11 was still in the air and possibly headed toward Washington. Only when NORAD contacted the FAA's Washington center did a manager mention, "We also lost American 77." It was already 9:34. Two minutes later, at 9:36, the FAA reported to NORAD that they had sighted an unidentified aircraft closing in on Washington, "six miles southeast of the White House. . . . deviating away." Flight 77 hit the Pentagon at 9:38.[77]

UNITED AIRLINES FLIGHT 93, the fourth hijacked plane, was also headed toward Washington, unbeknownst to anyone at NORAD. Flight 93 had taken off from Newark Airport at 8:42 a.m., more than half an hour behind schedule. It was not hijacked until 9:28. In viewing the timeline of events aboard Flight 93, the consequences of the airlines and FAA's inaction on 9/11 becomes clearer than ever. American Airlines, the FAA, and even the military knew about the hijacking of Flight 11 before Flight 93 even left the ground. Before its cockpit was taken over, two planes had hit the World Trade Center, and the hijackers' intentions were clear. But, as the *9/11 Report* says, "As news of the hijackings filtered through the FAA and the airlines, it does not seem to have occurred to their leadership that they needed to alert other aircraft in the air that they too might be at risk."[78]

The report continues, "FAA controllers at Boston Center, which had tracked the first two hijackings, requested at 9:07 that [the FAA's] Herndon Command Center 'get messages to airborne aircraft to increase security for the cockpit.' There is no evidence that Herndon took such action." If they had, they clearly might have saved Flight 93 from being hijacked. "Several FAA air traffic control officials told us it was the air carriers' responsibility to notify their planes of security problems. . . . that it was simply not the FAA's place to order the airlines what to tell their pilots." In another example of spectacularly understated prose, the 9/11 Commission remarked, "We believe such statements do not reflect an adequate appreciation of the FAA's responsibility for the safety and security of civil aviation."[79]

The 9/11 Commission found "no evidence . . . that American Airlines ever sent any cockpit warnings to its aircraft on 9/11. United's first decisive action to notify its airborne aircraft to take defensive action did not come until 9:19, when a United flight dispatcher . . . took the initiative to begin transmitting warnings to his 16 intercontinental flights: 'Beware any cockpit intrusion. Two a/c [aircraft] hit World Trade Center.'" His warning reached Flight 93 at 9:24. At 9:26, the pilot responded and asked for confirmation. But two minutes later, controllers in Cleveland heard shouts from the cockpit: "Hey, get out of here—get out of here—get out of here." The pilot had heard the warning, but had not had time to react before the hijackers entered the cockpit.[80]

On 9/11, there was only one group of people who were aware

of the earlier hijackings and used their knowledge to take decisive and effective action: the passengers on Flight 93. After the hijacking, as on the other three hijacked planes, passengers and crew began calling friends and family on the ground. They learned of the attacks on the World Trade Center; then they talked among themselves. And then, as the *9/11 Commission Report* put it, "They decided, and acted."[81]

This was in stark contrast to the FAA, which knew about the hijacking of Flight 93 soon after it took place and continued to track the plane closely, but did not notify the military, even after its controllers at Cleveland suggested they do so. At 9:46, the FAA Command Center notified FAA headquarters in Washington that the plane was now "twenty-nine minutes out of Washington, D.C." Three minutes later, they had the following conversation:

> COMMAND CENTER: Uh, do we want to think, about, uh, about scrambling aircraft?
> FAA HEADQUARTERS: Oh, God, I don't know.
> COMMAND CENTER: Uh, that's a decision somebody's gonna have to make probably in the next ten minutes.
> FAA HEADQUARTERS: Uh, ya know everybody just left the room.[82]

As the 9/11 Commission reports, "Despite the discussions about military assistance, no one at FAA headquarters requested military assistance regarding United 93. Nor did any manager at FAA headquarters pass any of the information it had about United 93 to the military."[83] It was the Cleveland control center that finally notified NEADS at 10:07. It also appears that the FAA took its time notifying potential targets in Washington—even after the Pentagon was hit. In the White House bunker, it was 10:02 before the Secret Service first told Dick Cheney that it had learned from the FAA of a plane headed toward Washington (and Cheney ordered it shot down). (See chapter 2.) But just as this was happening, the unarmed passengers on Flight 93 were wrestling their plane to the gound in a Pennsylvania field.

WHERE ARE THEY NOW?

While the fires still burned at Ground Zero, the airline lobbyists swung into action to engineer an enormous bailout for the industry. As Andrew Thomas describes in *Aviation Insecurity*, a veritable army descended upon Capitol Hill: Linda Daschle, former Republican National Committee chairman Haley Barbour, former Reagan administration official (and wife of a California congressman) Rebecca Cox—they were all there, twenty-seven in-house lobbyists working together with lobbyists from forty-two different law firms. "Leading the charge were several airline CEOs, many of whom were big contributors to the Bush campaign in 2000." Within a week of 9/11, they were testifying before the House Committee on Transportation and Infrastructure, asking for billions in handouts and loan guarantees.[84]

Commercial aviation had been shut down—all planes grounded—for three days following the 9/11 attacks. This shutdown certainly cost the airlines money—$340 million a day, according to the industry's analysis, for a total of just over a billion dollars. Yet the airlines asked Congress for $5 billion in immediate cash, along with a slew of loan guarantees and protective legislation.[85]

Ten days after 9/11, Congress gave them what they wanted. In record time, it passed a bill granting the airlines $5 billion outright and $10 billion in guaranteed loans. The industry also got guarantees that the government would pick up the added costs of insurance premiums. And under the new legislation the federal government—not the airlines—would pay for much of the cost of air security throughout the nation. This was a boon to the airlines, which were paying some $1.2 billion in security costs every year. The government would now pay for all the security measures that the airlines, with their powerful lobbies, had resisted for years, including reinforced cockpit doors and better screening devices.[86]

The industry promised an accounting to the Department of Transportation for all the money spent. But based on the history of the airlines' relationship with the FAA and the DOT, this was a case of the fox guarding the henhouse. The Government Accounting Office, however, later estimated that the airlines had overprojected their losses from 9/11 by $5 billion.[87]

Even the bill's victims compensation fund, which President Bush said would "help the victims and their families," was designed to protect the airlines. Under the legislation, the families of those killed on the ground and in the hijacked planes, as well as people injured in the attacks, had two choices: they could give up the right to sue the airlines and instead receive a share of public funds set aside for victims compensation—or they could reserve the right to sue and take their chances in court.[88]

The bill passed in the House by a seven-to-one majority. One of the few holdouts, California Democrat George Miller, remarked on the success of the airlines' whirlwind lobbying campaign: "The big dog got the bone. After September 11, the mood was one of shared sacrifice. People had lost their jobs and their lives. And the first thing that happened was the airline industry came in while everyone else is waiting to see if they can make their mortgage payments."[89] In the Senate there was only one opposing vote, Illinois Republican Peter Fitzgerald, who later said, "The only people who got bailed out were the shareholders. The one million airline employees were left twisting in the wind."[90] In fact, some in Congress had pressed for measures to help laid-off airline employees,

such as extending unemployment benefits and health-care coverage, but these provisions did not make it into the final bill.

Overall, the 9/11 attacks and their aftermath were a financial
blessing for the airlines. Ever since the stock market tanked in
2000, business travel had shriveled while fuel prices rose. Some
airlines were living on the edge before 9/11. The attacks gave
them some unexpected financial relief. With the legislation safely
in the can, they proceeded to fire some tens of thousands of
employees—20 percent of the workforce at most major airlines—and shut down numerous unprofitable routes, which they
had promised not to do.[91]

Congress then turned to the question of aviation security and,
in November, passed the Aviation and Transportation Security
Act. The legislation was held up for some time by the Bush
administration's resistance to making airport screeners federal
employees. (A compromise was reached that federalized workers
over the short term but denied them certain standard benefits and
rights, including whistle-blower protections.)

Under the new law, a special agency was created to oversee aviation security. The Transportation Security Administration (TSA)
was placed in charge of all security-related functions formerly
handled by the FAA and would oversee the improvements that
were supposed to take place over the next two years. There had
been debate over where to locate this agency. Some thought it
should be connected to other agencies responsible for national
security and law enforcement, possibly the Department of Justice. But the airlines and their allies argued that it should be
placed within the Department of Transportation, where their
long-standing influence lay—so that, of course, was where it
ended up.[92]

Two years after its creation, the TSA employed seventy thousand employees—almost triple the number originally projected—
and was the largest federal agency created since World War II. It

had spent $8 billion.[93] And the airlines were still complaining that security was costing them too much in money and time. Airline security had perhaps improved, but only marginally, and the agency had missed vital deadlines, such as a requirement that all checked baggage be screened by explosive detection devices no later than December 31, 2002. By the summer of 2005, Democrats on the House Committee on Homeland Security were complaining that more than one hundred progress reports were overdue from the Department of Homeland Security, including dozens from the TSA.[94]

And what about the FAA, now relieved of its security duties?

The only fallout from 9/11 at the FAA seems to have landed on Michael Canavan, the head of Civil Aviation Security, who quit two months after the attacks. A thirty-four-year veteran of the Army Special Forces, Canavan was generally considered a much stronger and more serious advocate for security than his predecessor, Cathal Flynn. Some FAA insiders said he had been forced out or quit in protest because his general desires for action were out of step with the FAA—or, in another account, because he refused to reassign air marshals from their assigned flights to planes carrying cabinet members, who were flying in a publicity stunt to help restore confidence in commercial air travel.[95]

Jane Garvey, who was in charge of the FAA on 9/11, moved on to a top job at APCO Worldwide, a "global communication consultancy," where her corporate biography on APCO's web site says: "Garvey's legacy as administrator includes leading the FAA through one of the toughest chapters in all of our history, restoring America's confidence in air travel, and strengthening airline safety. . . . Under the leadership of Jane F. Garvey, U.S. air travel is safer, more efficient, and the FAA is poised for continued success."

There is no public evidence showing that anyone at American Airlines or United Airlines was ever held responsible for his or her actions on 9/11—for security breaches, delays in reporting hijackings, or anything else. Nor is there evidence of any corporate accountability.

When United Airlines hired new CEO Glenn Tilton in the fall of 2002, it gave him a $3 million signing bonus and a $4.5 million retirement account.[96] A few months later, in December 2002, Tilton took the company into Chapter 11 bankruptcy, subsequently "slashing 24,000 jobs and wringing $3 billion from the remaining 58,000 workers' annual wages and benefits. [Tilton] almost single-handedly created a crisis of confidence in America's corporate pension system when he also dumped United's underfunded employee retirement plans, with their $6.6 billion in liabilities, into the lap of the federal government."[97] Much was made of Tilton's August 2004 salary reduction, from $845,500 to $712,500—but he later took a bonus of $366,000 for the year, even as he talked of needing additional employee pay cuts to get the airline out of bankruptcy. (It remained there as of August 2005.)[98]

American Airlines narrowly avoided bankruptcy in April 2003 by negotiating $1.6 billion in wage and benefit reductions with its employee unions. Its CEO, who had voluntarily given up bonuses and made only $811,000 in 2002, resigned during the negotiations after the unions learned that most management was retaining huge compensation packages. His replacement was none other than Gerard Arpey, the executive vice president who had been in charge at American headquarters on 9/11 and had learned of the hijackings after Betty Ong's phone call and failed to pass the information on to vital sources. When Arpey announced that he would forego any pay raise with his promotion, keeping his salary of $513,700, an American Airlines spokesperson said that Arpey had always believed in "shared sacrifice."[99]

As for the current state of commercial airline security, the most recent official assessment comes in a so-called confidential report leaked to the *New York Times* in early June 2005. The report asserts that air security could be improved with amazingly simple and relatively inexpensive steps to better screen both bags and people. These steps include such things as making longer tables on which passengers deposit their carry-on luggage while going through security checkpoints and locking exit doors through which deplaning passengers leave and through which any terrorist could walk aboard.

Some suggestions seem more than obvious, like having an armed guard at checkpoints. "If, say, a handgun were discovered," the report says, "the terrorist would have ample ability to retain control of it. Screeners are neither expecting to encounter a real weapon nor are they trained to gain control of it." The report apparently fails to specify the cost of the suggested changes to air security and does not say who would pay for them.[100]

This confidential study was prepared at the request of Congress but carried out by Northrop Grumman, the big defense contractor, and the staff of the Department of Homeland Security. Northrop Grumman has every incentive to be making studies like this one, because it is socked into the potentially large and lucrative homeland security business along with the other major Pentagon contractors. One of the company's major projects is to adapt its Guardian antimissile defense system for use on civilian commercial airliners, to protect against shoulder-fired surface-to-air missiles, long considered a terrorist weapon of choice. The company already has a Department of Homeland Security contract worth about $45 million to develop the antimissile system, with testing scheduled to begin in the summer of 2005. Installing the systems on all sixty-eight hundred U.S. commercial aircraft would cost $6 billion, according to Northrop Grumman's own estimate; a RAND Corporation study estimated the cost at closer to $11 billion.[101]

Northrop Grumman is also up to its eyeballs in politics. Within the defense industry, the Center for Responsive Politics reports, Northrop Grumman was the number two contributor to federal candidates and parties in the 2003–4 election cycle, second only to Lockheed Martin. Northrop Grumman contributed $1.688 million, nearly two-thirds of it to Republicans.[102]

A more informal—and scathing—assessment of the current state of air security comes from former Red Team member Steve Elson. For all the new bureaucracy and added expense, says Elson, the so-called regulators continue to place the needs of the airline industry before those of the passengers, and as long as this continues, little will change. "The facts remain the facts," said Elson from a vantage point of nearly four years after September 11, 2001. "It is still child's play to knock down fifty airplanes in a few hours' span with near 100 percent chance of success, and probably quite easy to fly a plane into the White House or Congress."[103]

The FAA, the government agency responsible for aviation security, played the role of spectator on 9/11. The only exception was a handful of relatively low-level FAA employees, who, in the absence of leadership, acted on their own initiative—the Boston controllers who called Otis Air Force Base themselves and the Cleveland dispatcher who warned his pilots to lock their cockpit doors.

At the airlines, the story was the same. Two of the largest U.S. carriers did little to save their passengers and crew. They placed them at risk by virtue of their lax security measures—with the assent of the FAA and in spite of repeated warnings. Here, again, a few rank-and-file individuals tried to serve a nonexistent homeland defense by sending out warnings, even as they faced their own deaths. And, while the powers that be stood by, a group of ordinary passengers took it into their own hands to defend their country and their compatriots by wrestling their plane to the ground.

Since the 9/11 attacks, more whistle-blowers have, like Steve

Elson and the other Red Team veterans, come forward to try, once again, to alert a nation at risk about what is—and is not—happening in our airports and in our skies. But in the government leadership, in the 9/11 Commission, and even in much of the media, no one has been listening.

2

Why Didn't the Government Protect Us?

HOW THE UNITED STATES GOVERNMENT FAILED ITS CITIZENS
BEFORE, DURING, AND AFTER 9/11

"I am very aware of the cameras. I'm trying to absorb that knowledge. I have nobody to talk to. I'm sitting in the midst of a classroom with little kids, listening to a children's story, and I realize I'm the commander in chief and the country has just come under attack." This is how President George W. Bush described the inner working of his mind during his now-famous seven-minute coma, which followed the devastating news whispered in his ear on the morning of September 11, 2001: "A second plane hit the other tower, and America's under attack."[1]

At his inauguration, nine months earlier, Bush took the presidential oath of office. In doing so, he, like all presidents before him, entered into a covenant with the American people. As president, he swore to "preserve, protect, and defend" the Constitution of the United States. As commander in chief, he also implicitly promised to protect and defend U.S. residents. Other government officials take similar oaths and make their own promises.

These promises are never more vital than in times of national crisis. This is also the time when they are most directly put to the test. Yet on 9/11, the president and key members of the administration—most notably, the vice president and the secretary of defense—responded to the crisis with a mixture of incompetence and treachery.

To be fair, from the outset they were handicapped by errors and cover-ups further down the line, at the FAA and at the corporate offices of commercial airlines. It is a travesty that the president and other top national leaders learned that American Airlines Flight 11 had hit the World Trade Center as most Americans did—from CNN. But once they did know what was happening, they had neither the will nor the ability to fulfill their covenant with the American people.

What's more, they stood in the way of others who were more courageous and more qualified to deal with this national crisis. In a kind of reverse coup, they withheld power from the military and from knowledgeable civilian experts, and kept it in the hands of political operatives. They apparently disregarded the Constitution and the military chain of command to shield an inadequate president and an absent secretary of defense. And after doing all this, they failed to save the life of a single American.

But on 9/11, the Bush White House did manage to do what it has always done best. Before the last plane had been brought to the ground, they had begun covering their tracks and thinking about spin. And before the dust had begun to settle in New York, Virginia, and Pennsylvania, they were mining the tragedy for political capital.

WHERE WAS THE PRESIDENT?

In his televised address on the evening of 9/11, Bush said, "Immediately following the first attack, I implemented our government's emergency response plans." But by all accounts, Bush had not even begun his reading session at Booker Elementary School in Sarasota when he was told that Flight 11 had hit one of the Twin Towers. And like other members of his administration, he seems

to have been unfazed by the idea of a major passenger jet crashing into an American landmark—even accidentally—or of scores
of New Yorkers trapped in a burning high-rise. Bush would later
say that, while he was at the school, when he saw the first plan strike
he made the cavalier comment, "Well, there's one terrible pilot."
In reality, there was no live footage of the crash, and videos of the
event would not be shown until that evening—and, according to
the principal, the television at the school was not even plugged in.[2]

Bush began his classroom photo-op just as United Airlines
Flight 175 crashed into the second tower. At 9:06 a.m., the president was told of the second attack, but the news failed to kick-
start him into presidential mode. Even after emerging from his
reveries, he repaired to a nearby classroom, where he spoke on the
phone with Dick Cheney and others, but gave them no directives. He prepared some remarks and spoke briefly to students,
teachers, and reporters, thanking "the folks here at Booker Elementary School for their hospitality" before promising "to hunt down
and to find those folks who committed this act."[3] At almost precisely the moment Bush was making his speech, 9:30 a.m., hijackers were seizing the cockpit of United Flight 93, and air traffic
controllers at Dulles Airport were picking up American Flight 77
on their radar, thirty miles out from Washington and traveling at
500 mph.

Bush himself has stated that he made no decisions of any kind
before boarding Air Force One.[4] Even his destination was unde-
cided at that point. By some accounts, Bush argued with Cheney
and with Secret Service agents that he wanted to return to Washington—but not firmly enough, apparently, to make it happen.[5]
There were also accounts that there were "credible terrorist
threats" to Air Force One throughout the day, but no evidence of
such threats has ever emerged.[6]

Bush was told about Flight 77's crash into the Pentagon just
before boarding the plane, where he paused to wave to reporters. The

plane took off at 9:56, just as the passengers aboard Flight 93 began their heroic struggle to regain control of their plane, and minutes before the South Tower of the World Trade Center collapsed.

Aboard Air Force One, everything was conducted with the utmost secrecy. Even after a destination was established, no one was told where the plane was headed, not even the air traffic controllers, and Secret Service agents went through the plane removing batteries from reporters' cell phones. After some delay, an escort of military fighter planes arrived. And on Air Force One, at least, an armed guard was eventually stationed outside the cockpit.[7]

Measures such as these are taken in times of crisis not only to protect the personal safety of the president, but also to ensure the security of the commander in chief, so that he will be able to direct military operations and lead the nation out of danger. Air Force One is outfitted to function as a flying command post, which is what it should, at this point, have become. Bush later complained that he had communications problems throughout the day, telling the 9/11 Commission that he had to use a regular cell phone rather than a secure line to talk with Cheney and others in Washington.[8] In any case, there is no conclusive evidence that Bush made any decisions or gave any orders while on the plane— or, indeed, at any time that day.

At 11:45 a.m., Air Force One landed at Barksdale Air Force Base in Shreveport, Louisiana, and Bush was hustled, under armed escort, to a secure location. Bush took the opportunity to tape a brief speech to the nation, which was broadcast at 1:04 p.m. He also seems to have spent much of his time at Barksdale on the phone with Cheney, arguing about where he should go next. At this point, rescue workers had already begun searching the rubble of the collapsed World Trade Center towers, and U.S. airspace had been cleared of all civilian aircraft—a fact apparently known to the president. But there was still talk of threats to Air Force One, and the president was kept on the move.[9]

Air Force One next flew to Offutt Air Force Base, outside
Omaha, Nebraska, headquarters for U.S. Strategic Command.
This base has bunkers three stories deep, designed to withstand a
nuclear blast, with a state-of-the-art command and communications center. Bush arrived at 2:50 and was taken down the narrow
"bunny hole" to the command post. From here, deep underground, Bush finally settled in and conducted an hour-long
videoconference call with top officials in Washington.

Although U.S. air space had been cleared four hours earlier,
Bush did not leave Nebraska until 4:33, by which time authorities had cleared the last plane flying anywhere in the northern half
of the Western Hemisphere. In the following days, Dick Cheney,
White House advisor Karl Rove, and press secretary Ari Fleisher
would all repeat the story of a "credible threat to Airforce One
being phoned in on 9/11." Conservative columnist William
Safire, who on September 12 had criticized Bush for not returning to Washington, was quickly informed by a "high White
House official" that a "threatening message received by the Secret
Service was relayed to the agents with the president that 'Air Force
One is next,'" and that "American code words were used showing
a knowledge of procedures that made the threat credible." Safire
reported that this information was confirmed by Rove, who told
him Bush had wanted to return to Washington, but the Secret
Service "informed him that the threat contained language that
was evidence that the terrorists had knowledge of his procedures
and whereabouts." Two weeks later, news reports revealed there was
no evidence that such a call was ever received, and the White
House gently backed away from the story.[10]

In fact, Bush may not have been entirely idle during his day of
flying from one underground bunker to another. While he apparently had little or no role in shaping the events of the day, he
seems to have given some thought to how those events could be
used to shape future foreign policy. Or perhaps his advisors and

speechwriters did. The president finally arrived back in Washington at 6:54, and at 8:30 he was on television, delivering a speech that already began to lay out like what some would come to call the "Bush Doctrine." He declared, "We will make no distinction between the terrorists who committed these acts and those who harbor them"—paving the way for the United States to make war on other nations in the name of the war on terror.

Shortly afterwards, in a 9:00 p.m. meeting with the National Security Council, he repeated this statement. According to former terrorism "czar" Richard Clarke, in his book *Against All Enemies*, Bush also said, "Everything is available for pursuit of this war. Any barriers in your way, they're gone." As Clarke tells it, when Donald Rumsfeld, of all people, wondered about violating international law, Bush yelled, "No. I don't care what the international lawyers say, we are going to kick some ass."[11]

WHO WAS IN CHARGE?

Presidential power is supposed to reside not in the Oval Office, but with the man, wherever he happens to be—whether in a remote military bunker or an elementary school classroom or in the skies aboard Air Force One. But if any locus of government power existed on 9/11, it was not with President Bush, but rather in the Presidential Emergency Operations Center (PEOC), the bunker beneath the East Wing of the White House, where Vice President Dick Cheney arrived shortly before 10:00 a.m.[12]

Cheney was not alone in the PEOC. But those few who should have had a voice in the decision-making process appear to have remained, for the most part, silent, deferring in all things to the vice president. Secretary of Transportation Norman Minetta, who had oversight of the FAA, made his way to the bunker but didn't do much there. He later told the 9/11 Commission that he had ordered all planes grounded at 9:45. But this decision was actually made independently by FAA National Operations Manager Ben Sliney, who was in his first day on the job.[13] Condoleeza Rice, always highly political and extremely deferential for a national security adviser, remained low-key during what should have been a pivotal moment for her office.

The others who joined Cheney in the PEOC were not experts on terrorism, national security, civilian aviation, or military tactics, but a group of key right-wing political operatives. They included conservative media celebrity and then White House "counselor" Mary Matalin and longtime Bush campaign crony and White House Communications Director Karen Hughes. Rounding out the group were Cheney's chief of staff, Scooter Libby, a leading neocon foreign policy strategist and architect of the Project for a New American Century, and his wife, Lynne Cheney, a powerful conservative ideologue, lately of the American Enterprise Institute, who was escorted to her husband's side by the Secret Service.

According to Richard Clarke, the PEOC was connected by telephone to a videoconference going on in the West Wing's Situation Room, which would at various points include high-ranking officials from all of the key players the Defense and State Departments, Joint Chiefs of Staff, attorney general's office, CIA, FBI, and FAA—as well as the counterterrorism "czar" himself. Within half an hour of the second WTC attack, teleconferences had also been established by the FAA and the Pentagon's National Military Command Center (NMCC).

According to the 9/11 Commission, "Because none of these teleconferences—at least before 10:00—included the right officials from both the FAA and Defense Department, none succeeded in meaningfully coordinating the military and FAA response to the hijackings."[14] The *9/11 Report* pays surprisingly little attention— and gives only a few lines of ink—to Clarke's West Wing teleconference, and which seems to have been the best equipped to deal with a crisis of this kind, and which might conceivably have taken more meaningful action, if empowered to do so. But power evidently resided in the hands of the far more political group gathered in the East Wing's PEOC, and that group seems also to have little use for Clarke's gathering. In his book, Clarke reports that someone in the PEOC later told him that attempts to listen in on the West Wing videoconference on speakerphone were impeded "because Mrs. Cheney keeps turning down the volume on you so she can hear CNN . . . and the vice president keeps hanging up the open line to you."[15]

The central decision faced by whoever took command that day, after the WTC attacks were a known fact, was a momentous one: Should the United States military be ordered to shoot down commercial airplanes full of civilian passengers, so that they, too, would not be used as missiles, most likely, it appeared, against targets in Washington, D.C.? This decision was indeed made, and the orders were given (though for various reasons, they were never carried out). These orders were given by the vice president of the United States, Dick Cheney.

Under the law, in this or any other crisis requiring a military response, the decision to engage the military must be made by the president, as commander in chief. He gives his orders to the secretary of defense, who is supposed to implement these orders by passing them on to the relevant battle commands—in this case, the North American Aerospace Defense Command (NORAD), which is responsible for defending American airspace and directs the Northeast Air Defense Sector (NEADS). Military actions might then be overseen by the National Military Command Center (NMCC). But the orders to engage would have to come from the president or the secretary of defense.[16]

In this chain of command, the vice president has no place whatsoever. According to the Twenty-Fifth Amendment to the Constitution, the vice president could claim such a place only if

the president were for some reason "unable to discharge the powers and duties of his office"—and even then, only with the support of the cabinet and the concurrence of Congress. It is unlikely
that the authors of the Twenty-Fifth Amendment, who codified
these detailed rules in the wake of the Kennedy assassination, were
thinking of simple presidential ineptitude or of poor cell-phone
reception.

It is equally unlikely that Dick Cheney could be ignorant of
these rules, or of the laws clearly specifying the chain of command. The military chain of command is not some remote or
obscure formula. Long on the books, it was reinforced and clarified in the Goldwater-Nichols Department of Defense Reorgani-
zation Act of 1986, debated and passed while Cheney was a
member of Congress. Cheney also served as secretary of defense
under the first George Bush—and surely would have paled at the
thought of Dan Quayle giving orders to shoot down planes.

But Vice President Cheney did, in fact, issue orders for military fighters to shoot down commercial jets on the morning of
September 11. He told the 9/11 Commission, and has repeatedly
told others, that he was authorized by the president in advance to
give these orders. Evidence of this prior authorization is thin and
contradictory. Even the carefully worded account in the *9/11
Commission Report* leaves ample room for doubt, although it stops
short of conclusions or accusations.

According to the *9/11 Commission Report*, Bush and Cheney
kept in touch that morning "not by an open line of communication, but through a series of calls." The report says Bush told the
Commission he was "frustrated with poor communications that
morning. He could not reach key officials, including Secretary
Rumsfeld, for a period of time. The line to the White House shel-
ter conference room—and the vice president—kept cutting off."[17]

Cheney told the Commission that he placed a call to Bush just
before 10:00 a.m., when he arrived in the PEOC bunker—about

the same time that Air Force One took off. Cheney said that the Air Force was trying to set up a combat air patrol (CAP) over Washington, and that he called to establish the rules of engagement for the CAP. Cheney reported telling Bush that the pilots would need authority "to shoot if the plane did not divert. He said the president signed off on that concept. The president said he remembered such a conversation, and that it reminded him of when he had been an interceptor pilot. The president emphasized to us that he had authorized the shootdown of hijacked aircraft."[18]

The only person who remembers hearing the vice president speak to the president at that time is the ever-faithful Condoleeza Rice. She testified to the Commission that she "remembered hearing him inform the president, 'Sir, the CAPS are up. Sir, they're going to want to know what to do.' Then she recalled hearing him say, 'Yes, Sir.'"[19]

Press accounts have quoted Bush's own later recollections of the conversation, held while he was on Air Force One. After Cheney recommended that he authorize the shootdowns, "I said, 'You bet.' There was a little discussion, but not much."[20]

The Commission delicately concluded: "Among the sources that reflect other important events of that morning, there is no documentary evidence for this call, but the relevant sources are incomplete." They added that others surrounding the vice president, including his chief of staff and his wife, "did not note a call between the president and Vice President" at that time. According to one report in *Newsweek*, some of the Commission's staff "flat out didn't believe the call ever took place" and expressed their skepticism in an early draft of their staff report. And one staff member said that pressure from the White House had led to the report being "watered down."[21]

Shortly after 10:10 a.m., the bunker began receiving reports of a plane headed for Washington. These reports came from the Secret Service, which was getting information directly from the

FAA—incorrect information, as it turned out, since the aircraft in question was Flight 93, which at that moment was wobbling through the skies over western Pennsylvania as its passengers fought their hijackers for control. Flight 93 had already crashed by the time an aide told Cheney it was only eighty miles away and asked him to authorize a shootdown. According to the *9/11 Report*, Cheney's "reaction was described by Scooter Libby as quick and decisive, 'in about the time it takes a batter to decide to swing.'" Cheney repeated the order a few minutes later, after hearing that the plane was now sixty miles out.

The only recorded challenge of any kind to Cheney's conduct that day came from Joshua Bolton, then the White House deputy chief of staff. Bolton told the Commission that he "watched the exchanges and, after what he called 'a quiet moment,' suggested that the vice president get in touch with the president and confirm the engage order. Bolton told us he wanted to make sure the president was told that the vice president had executed the order. He said he had not heard any prior discussion on the subject with the president." Cheney made the call at 10:18. This after-the-fact call, unlike earlier communications, is well documented. Bush, of course, concurred with Cheney's decision.[22]

Whether they were made legally or not, Cheney's orders came too late. The passengers on Flight 93 had already done what their government had failed to do: they had brought down their plane and sacrificed their own lives in order to protect their nation's capital and their compatriots on the ground. In any case, Cheney's orders were never received by the pilots over Washington. This is perhaps just as well. At about 10:30, Cheney got word of another plane just five miles away and immediately gave orders to "take it out." The vice president, as it later turned out, had commanded military fighter jets to shoot down a low-flying Medevac helicopter.[23]

In an intricate dance around this subject, the 9/11 Commission quietly raised doubts but fell short of drawing conclusions or making accusations. What makes the matter especially difficult to resolve is the refusal of both the president and the vice president to address under oath what they did that morning. After at first refusing altogether to talk to the Commission and then haggling over terms, Bush agreed to meet with the Commission members at the White House. The deal dictated that Cheney be there with him, that no notes could be taken, that no transcript of the session be made, and that no public record of any kind be issued. Neither Bush nor Cheney would testify under oath; their meeting with the Commission has been characterized as a conversation.

As any cop in the land knows, people who are telling the truth don't behave this way, and evidence gathered through such a "conversation" isn't worth much. But the 9/11 Commission had clearly pressed the issue as far as it was collectively willing to do. Only two pages of the Commission's final report are devoted to this question. And the account is often circumstantial, relying (as does much of the report) on media reports, rather than sworn testimony—the overall effect of which is to make the subject even more murky. Some of the commissioners were clearly interested in protecting political allies. But one imagines, too, a reluctance to pursue a truth that might result in the discrediting of the president and the impeachment of the vice president, layering, in effect, a constitutional crisis on top of a national tragedy.

In a practical sense, one could argue that it makes little difference whether or not Cheney received the president's authorization to order the military shootdown of civilian planes. It should come as no surprise to anyone that when the chips were down, it was Dick Cheney who was the real decision-maker. Even Bush himself, apparently, does not claim to have done anything more decisive than say "You bet" to Cheney's request. Cheney was in charge, and he had little use for anyone's advice. He watched CNN with his wife, and then he made the decision to "take it out."

The president's basic inability to serve as commander in chief may be the unspoken truth at the root of these events. But it certainly matters, as well, that in a time of crisis, the Constitution may have been ignored. It matters that established laws concerning military action seem to have been disregarded—and in fact, that the role of the military itself, and of an expert civil service, seems to have been swept aside in the atmosphere of a palace coup.

WHERE WAS THE SECRETARY OF DEFENSE?

Considering he was the man charged with defending the United States and overseeing its armed forces, Secretary of Defense Donald Rumsfeld spent an astonishingly aimless morning on September 11, 2001. As the nation fell under attack, neither Rumsfeld himself nor his top administration colleagues seem to have felt that he needed to be involved in essential decision-making. He received little information from the White House and the military, was missing in action from vital meetings and conference calls, and remained unaware that his own headquarters were in danger until he felt the impact as the plane hit.

The image of Rumsfeld standing in the Pentagon's parking lot, watching the building burn and his staff members being carried away on stretchers, is an apt reflection of his overall role on 9/11. On the day when his country most needed defending, he was a spectator. Or, as the 9/11 Commission politely put it, the better part of the morning had passed before the secretary of defense even began "gaining situational awareness."[24]

Rumsfeld later sought to justify his position, testifying to the 9/11 Commission that he actually had no responsibility for what happened that day. An attack within U.S. borders by a civilian aircraft was, he said, "a law enforcement matter to be handled by law enforcement authorities," and not by the Department of Defense. In fact, it is not clear what Rumsfeld believed his role was that day or even where he was for long periods of crucial time.

What *is* clear is that even while the country remained under attack, Rumsfeld's mind was elsewhere. He was thinking not of Osama Bin Laden and Al Qaeda, but of Iraq and Saddam Hussein—a man with whom he'd had a mercurial relationship for more than twenty years.

By Rumsfeld's own account to the 9/11 Commission, on the morning of September 11 he was having breakfast with members of Congress. "Someone handed me a note," he reported, "saying a plane had hit one of the World Trade Center towers. Shortly thereafter, I was in my office with a CIA briefer and I was told that a second plane had hit the other tower. Shortly thereafter, at 9:38, the Pentagon shook with an explosion of then unknown origin."[25]

Like other top government and military officials, Rumsfeld first learned of the crisis from the news media. But even after the second plane hit the Twin Towers at 9:03, Rumsfeld took no action to protect U.S. territory or citizens from further attacks. During the following thirty-five minutes—a time period that he dismissed with the phrase "shortly thereafter"—Rumsfeld apparently sat in his office receiving briefings. He didn't move until a plane hit his own building.

Rumsfeld and his Pentagon colleagues had received no warning that the hijacked Flight 77 was bearing down on the Washington, D.C., area. But considering the fact that he was sitting in his office being briefed on the World Trade Center attacks, the secretary of defense was surprisingly mystified when the Pentagon "shook with an explosion of then unknown origin." It is strange, too, that Rumsfeld's next choice was to walk outside and see for himself what had happened on the opposite side of the building, more than two thousand feet from his office, rather than repairing to the National Military Command Center (NMCC), just two hundred feet away, where a vital teleconference had already been initiated by key Pentagon officials. As Rumsfeld himself described it, "I don't know what made me do anything I did, to be honest with you. I just do it instinctive. I looked out the window, saw nothing here, and then went down the hallway until the smoke was too bad, then to a stairwell down." Once he reached the site, Rumsfeld said, he "asked a person who'd seen it, and he told me that a plane had hit it."[26]

What Rumsfeld did next is the subject of some controversy. He described spending time aiding the wounded at the crash site. "Then, at some moment I decided I should be in here [his office] figuring out what to do, because your brain begins to connect things."[27] To the 9/11 Commission, he simply reported, "I went outside to determine what had happened. I was not there long because I was back in the Pentagon with a crisis action team shortly before or after 10:00 a.m." But according to numerous accounts, including the *9/11 Report*, Rumsfeld did not arrive at the NMCC until "shortly before 10:30."[28]

The exact whereabouts and activities of the secretary of defense in between the Pentagon attack at 9:37 and his arrival at the NMCC fifty minutes later take on special significance in light of what was happening during that time—and what wasn't happening. During this crucial period, Flight 93 was speeding toward Washington. Because of the incompetence of the FAA, neither the NMCC nor the White House knew about Flight 93 until 10:00—about the same time its own passengers were wrestling it to the ground. (In fact, they had been spending their time tracking an entirely different plane.) But Donald Rumsfeld had no reason to believe there *weren't* more hijacked jets in the sky, heading for additional targets and demanding a military response. Nor could the secretary of defense have been ignorant of his position in the military chain of command.

If what Rumsfeld did that morning remains a mystery, what he was supposed to be doing is abundantly clear. "On September 11, the normal scramble-approved procedure was for an FAA official to contact the [NMCC] and request Pentagon air support.

Someone in the NMCC would call NORAD's command center and ask about availability of aircraft, then seek approval from the Defense Secretary—Donald H. Rumsfeld—to launch fighters."[29] Rumsfeld, second only to the president, was responsible for issuing the orders that would scramble fighters to shoot down a hijacked aircraft. Even if the orders came directly from the president, the secretary of defense would likely need to clarify and interpret these orders. He would need to establish clear rules of engagement that could be passed on to the relevant military commands, allowing them to execute the orders quickly and effectively. Without Rumsfeld, the chain of command was missing an irreplaceable link.

If Rumsfeld seems to have forgotten or dismissed his critical role, so, too, apparently, did the president and vice president. Rumsfeld told the 9/11 Commission that when he returned from the crash site, "I had one or more calls in my office, one of which was with the president." In another one of its restrained paragraphs, the Commission report summarizes, "In most cases, the chain of command authorizing the use of force runs from the president to the secretary of defense and from the secretary to the combatant commander. The president apparently spoke to Secretary Rumsfeld for the first time that morning shortly after 10:00. No one can recall the content of this conversation, but it was a brief call in which the subject of shootdown authorization was not discussed."[30]

The omission is all the more strange in light of Bush and Cheney's other statements regarding shootdown orders. Bush had told the 9/11 Commission that just before 10:00—thus, according to the president's own timeline, not long before his conversation with Rumsfeld—he had spoken to Cheney and had authorized the shootdown of hijacked planes. Long after the conversation took place, Bush claimed to remember it clearly, saying that it had "reminded him of when he had been an interceptor pilot." But evidently, he didn't remember to tell the secretary of defense about the conversation moments after it happened.

More familiar with chain of command, the NMCC cared more about Rumsfeld's participation. A conference had been convened there at 9:29, and at 9:37, the NMCC (which was undamaged by the Pentagon attack) initiated an "Air Threat Conference Call," which would continue for most of the day. [31]

At 9:39, the officer handling the teleconference requested that the secretary of defense be added to the call. But by this time, Rumsfeld had already left his nearby office and was heading outside to investigate the "explosion of then unknown origin."

When Rumsfeld at last arrived at the NMCC at 10:30, he began "gaining situational awareness," joining the Air Threat Conference Call. "One of the first exchanges was with the vice president," Rumsfeld told the 9/11 Commission. "He informed me of the president's authorization to shoot down hostile aircraft coming to Washington, D.C." By this time, Dick Cheney has already ordered the shootdown of Flight 93 and of a stray Medevac helicopter; he told Rumsfeld, erroneously, that the order had been transmitted to the pilots and "they've already taken a couple of aircraft out."[32]

Rumsfeld didn't question the chain of command, but he did express the need to make sure that the pilots had a clear understanding of their rules of engagement. "It may well be the first time in history that U.S. armed forces in peacetime have been given the authority to fire on fellow Americans going about their lawful business," Rumsfeld told the Commission. He did not seem concerned that this momentous decision had been made without his approval, participation, or knowledge.

Once he was in the loop, Rumsfeld continued "to work to refine the standing rules of engagement"; a final version of the rules was circulated at about 1:00, three hours after the last hijacked plane had crashed. "I spent the remainder of the morning and the afternoon,"

Rumsfeld said, "participating in the air threat conference, talking to the president, the vice president, General Myers [acting chairman of the Joint Chiefs of Staff] and others and thinking about the way forward."[33]

Three years later, reflecting on that day's events in his testimony before the 9/11 Commission, Rumsfeld would present a novel explanation for his lack of leadership—or even of involvement—on September 11. He argued that the Department of Defense was not responsible for defending the nation within its national boundaries. Rumsfeld had the following exchange with Commission member Richard Ben-Veniste:

> RUMSFELD: Let me put something into some context. The Department of Defense, as Senator [Bob] Kerrey has indicated earlier, did not have responsibility for the borders. It did not have responsibility for the airports.
> BEN-VENISTE: I understand that.
> RUMSFELD: And the fact that I might not have known something ought not to be considered unusual. Our task was to be oriented out of this country. . . .
> BEN-VENISTE: I understand that.
> RUMSFELD: . . . and to defend against attacks from abroad. And a civilian aircraft was a law enforcement matter to be handled by law enforcement authorities and aviation authorities. And that is the way our government was organized and arranged. So those questions you're posing are good ones. And they are valid, and they ought to be asked. But they ought to be asked of people who had the statutory responsibility for those things.

In an exchange with Jamie Gorelick, another Commission member, Rumsfeld further elaborated on this point: "First let me respond as to what the responsibility of the Department of Defense has been with a hijacking. As I said, it was a law enforcement issue. And the Department of Defense has had various understandings with [the] FAA whereby when someone squawks 'hijack,' they have an arrangement with the Department of Defense that the military would send an airplane up and monitor the flight, but certainly in a hijack situation, [the Defense Department] did not have authority to shoot down a plane that was being hijacked."

Even with his reputation for fantastic and unfounded statements, Rumsfeld outdid himself in these statements, which are contradicted by other parts of his testimony, as well as by fact and by law. The Commission, however, failed to press the matter, so we may never know what Rumsfeld envisioned as the appropriate response by "law enforcement" to the 9/11 attacks. (NYPD SWAT teams on the roofs of skyscrapers? FBI agents with shoulder-to-air missiles on the Washington Mall?)

The secretary of defense may have been sitting in his office or wandering outside the Pentagon while the country was under attack. But once the dust began to settle, and it was time to start "thinking about the way foreword," Rumsfeld showed himself more than ready to take an active role. In the geography of Donald Rumsfeld's mind, the road to Baghdad was paved with the ashes of the World Trade Center.

While Rumsfeld was still in the Pentagon parking lot, at 9:53, the National Security Agency had intercepted a call from a Bin Laden operative in Afghanistan to a person in the former Soviet republic of Georgia. The caller said he had "heard good news" and another target was still to be hit (apparently, by the plane that was brought down in the Pennsylvania countryside). This was the first firm indication the government had that Bin Laden was behind the attack.

Two hours later, at 12:05, CIA Director George Tenet told Rumsfeld about the NSA intercept. As reported by CBS News, based on leaked notes from the NMCC conference, the secretary of defense was surprisingly reluctant to make much of the call: "Rumsfeld felt it was 'vague,' that it 'might not mean something,' and that there was 'no good basis for hanging hat.' In other words, the evidence was not clear-cut enough to justify military action against Bin Laden."

Later in the afternoon, the CIA reported that passenger manifests for the hijacked planes showed that at least three of the hijackers were suspected Al Qaeda operatives. According to the leaked notes obtained by CBS, Rumsfeld learned that "One guy is associate of Cole bomber"—the Al Qaeda suicide bomber who attacked the U.S. warship in Yemen in 2000. At 2:40, the notes report Rumsfeld beginning to take aim at the target his heart truly desires. He wants the "best info fast. Judge whether good enough hit S.H. [Saddam Hussein] at same time. Not only UBL [Osama Bin Laden]. Go massive. Sweep it all up. Things related and not."[36]

This was the first indication that Rumsfeld was disregarding specific intelligence clearly linking the attack to Al Qaeda, and instead had begun to fantasize about getting Saddam Hussein. Not five hours after the attacks had ended, the secretary of defense was thinking about how to exploit the deaths of nearly three thousand Americans to pursue his larger foreign policy aims, whether "related or not." For Rumsfeld, this was "thinking about the way forward."

Some twelve hours later, in the early hours of September 12, Richard Clarke returned to the White House after a brief break for another round of meetings on the crisis, but, "Instead, I walked into a series of discussions about Iraq." In a well-known passage from his book *Against All Enemies*, Clarke writes, "At first

I was incredulous that we were talking about something other than getting al Qaeda. Then I realized with almost a sharp physical pain that Rumsfeld and [Deputy Defense Secretary] Wolfowitz were going to try to take advantage of this national tragedy to promote their agenda about Iraq."[37]

Clarke asserts that "since the beginning of the administration, indeed well before, they had been pressing for a war with Iraq." In fact, Donald Rumsfeld's focus had been on Iraq, in one way or another, for more than twenty years.

Rumsfeld's contact with Saddam Hussein had begun in the early 1980s. At that time, the Reagan administration was worried that the revolutionaries of the Islamic republic of Iran would best the Iraqis on the field of battle, thus opening the Middle East and Israel to Iranian attacks—and, more to the point, endanger oil shipments. Reagan needed someone to cozy up to Saddam Hussein, and he called upon Rumsfeld, the former White House chief of staff and defense secretary (under Gerald Ford) who was at that time serving as president and CEO of the pharmaceutical giant G. D. Searle.

Rumsfeld traveled to Baghdad as a special presidential envoy to the Middle East and was photographed shaking hands with Saddam. The visit was the beginning of an already well-documented relationship between Baghdad and Washington that would last through the rest of the 1980s. American aid channels to Iraq, previously cut off, were reopened, and Saddam began to receive economic support, intelligence, and equipment and parts that could be used in warfare. It has long been believed, though never conclusively proved, that the United States sent Iraq components that were used to create germ and biological weapons that were used against the Iranian front lines.

There had been some talk, during this same period, of former Reagan administration officials becoming involved in a proposed scheme to pipe Iraqi oil to Israel. But the deal fell through. In

1986, with the Iran-Iraq war expanding, Iraq sought to protect its oil tankers by reflagging them as Kuwaiti. The Iranians kept on bombing the ships. Then the Soviet Union offered to put Soviet naval vessels in the Persian Gulf. The United States rushed to stave off the move by reflagging the ships as American. If the ships were attacked, then the U.S. Navy would respond. To protect Saddam Hussein's ships, operating under our flag, the Pentagon stationed large numbers of warships in the Persian Gulf.[38]

So Rumsfeld had intimate knowledge of Saddam Hussein, and helped set in motion a policy of support for Saddam's regime that went so far as to shield his tankers with American military forces and with the U.S. flag. Along with his friends in the Reagan-Bush-Bush dynasty, Rumsfeld must have felt intense betrayal and outrage when their old ally Saddam dared to invade Kuwait. The will toward retribution, combined with a larger desire to enhance American influence, were apparently enough to make him build a case for a war against Iraq on the backs of thousands of dead American civilians.

Rumsfeld was not, of course, alone in this inclination—though he seems to have been either the most virulent or just the least tactful about his intentions. As Richard Clarke recalls in his book, "By the afternoon on Wednesday [September 12], Secretary Rumsfeld was talking about broadening the objectives of our response and 'getting Iraq.'" Clarke says Rumsfeld suggested that "having been attacked by Al Qaeda, for us now to go bombing Iraq in response would be like our invading Mexico after the Japanese attacked us at Pearl Harbor."

Later that day, Clarke writes, "Secretary Rumsfeld complained that there were no decent targets. At first I thought Rumsfeld was joking. But he was serious and the president did not reject out of hand the idea of attacking Iraq. Instead, he noted that what we needed to do with Iraq was to change the government, not just hit it with more cruise missiles, as Rumsfeld had implied."[39] Within thirty-six hours of the attacks, the Bush administration's agenda was complete, and the way ahead was clear.

WHY COULDN'T THE MILITARY STOP IT?

For many in the United States and around the world, it came as no surprise that the likes of Rumsfeld, Cheney, and Bush responded inadequately, incompetently, and even illegally in the face of a true national crisis. What might have been less expected is the failure of the U.S. military to provide any meaningful defense against attacks of this magnitude on American soil.

The rank-and-file men and women of the U.S. armed forces are undoubtedly courageous and willing to act. And we are used to thinking of the American military as well funded, well equipped, and well trained. How is it, then, that they were unable to protect the American people from a dozen fanatics with box cutters?

The answer lies in two basic sets of facts. First, despite a mammoth defense budget and state-of-the-art equipment, the American military was stunningly ill prepared, on 9/11, to respond to an attack within the continental United States. Second, the relevant military commands received neither the information nor the orders they would have needed to mount a swift and effective defense against the attacks. Thinly scattered as they were, the forces deployed on the East Coast might have been able to stop one or more of the planes. But no one told them what was going on, and no one instructed them what to do, until it was far too late.

Beginning with the advent of the Cold War more than fifty years ago, U.S. politicians voted billions upon billions of dollars for the most up-to-date defense system to protect America and its allies from the Soviet Union. From nuclear missiles and bombers down to grade school duck-and-cover civil defense drills, America was always preparing itself for the worst. In 1958, the United States and Canada jointly established NORAD, the

North American Aerospace Defense Command, charged with defending the airspace of North America and generally defending the continent from attack. At its Cold War height, twenty-six NORAD sites had multiple fighters constantly on alert, ready to respond to an air attack by the Soviets.

But when the Cold War ended and the Soviet Union and Eastern bloc broke apart, American domestic defenses were cut back drastically. On September 11, 2001, there were just seven alert sites in North America, each with two fighters prepared for immediate response.[40] New York and Washington were under the protection of NORAD's Northeast Air Defense Sector, headquartered in upstate New York, which in turn oversaw two alert sites—Otis Air Force Base on Cape Cod, Massachusetts, and Langley Air Force Base in Hampton, Virginia. This means that on 9/11, the nation's capital and its largest city—logically, its most likely targets—were defended by four fighter jets.

However, even if there had been dozens of alert fighters ready to take off, they would have had little chance of intercepting the hijacked planes on 9/11, for the simple reason that they did not know about them. With seemingly everyone else in aviation aware of the hijackings—from flight attendants to ground dispatchers to airline management to regional air controllers and eventually top FAA officials—the military organization charged with defending the American continent remained in the dark. Even after NORAD learned about the hijackings and the fighters were in the air, military commanders were receiving incomplete or incorrect information. During the critical moments, they also had no orders—and once they did, confusion over the chain of command and rules of engagement prevented them from executing these orders.

In short, on 9/11 the military's fighting forces were prevented from doing their job because others—at the airlines and the FAA, in the White House and the Pentagon—did not do their jobs. In fact, the only people who performed with any distinction that day were the passengers and crew aboard the doomed flights, who sent out a steady stream of distress calls, provided vital information, and even thwarted the final attack.

As detailed in chapter 1, these arguably criminal delays in conveying information about the hijackings were caused, for the most part, by the FAA and the private airlines. But a failure of such magnitude needs to be viewed from all angles, so it is worth revisiting, one more time, the actions of officials in Washington and their impact on military response.

The two men with authority to order military actions of the kind required on 9/11 were, again, President Bush and Secretary of Defense Rumsfeld. Neither one had any advance notice whatsoever of any of the hijackings. They learned about them, one by one, only after the planes had crashed. Based on their conduct that morning, however, it seems unlikely that they would have done much even if they had known. The actual decision-making still would have fallen, as it did, to Vice President Cheney, despite his position outside the military chain of command.

Cheney, too, lacked information about any of the hijackings until the planes were all down. He did, however, give orders to shoot down aircraft. This happened because, even after Flight 93 was on the ground, Cheney was receiving reports that it was speeding toward Washington—which it would still have been, had its own passengers not stopped it about ten minutes earlier.

Cheney's order to "take it out" was received by NORAD's Northeast Air Defense Sector in upstate New York (NEADS) just after 10:30. Transcripts of conversations at NEADS headquarters, as well as interviews by the 9/11 Commission, show "considerable confusion over the nature and effect of the order." The *9/11 Report* states, "The NEADS commander told us he did not pass along the order because he was unaware of its ramifications. . . . They did not pass the order to the fighters circling

Washington and New York because they were unsure how the pilots would, or should, proceed with this guidance. In short, while leaders in Washington believed that the fighters above them had been instructed to 'take out' hostile aircraft, the only orders actually conveyed to the pilots were to 'ID type and tail.'"[41]

The NEADS commanders knew that the engagement order came from Cheney, as the transcript shows: "Okay, you read that from the Vice President, right? Vice President has cleared. Vice President has cleared us to intercept traffic and shoot down if they do not respond."[42] One can only speculate whether their willingness to execute these orders was affected by their knowledge that the vice president had no authority to give them. What seems clearer is the fact that Cheney failed to provide any guidance on the rules of engagement. Rumsfeld might have done so, had he not been missing in action at the time. And the plentiful number of Pentagon brass at the NMCC were not being consulted by Cheney—and in any case, they might not have provided guidance for a shootdown order that had not been approved by Rumsfeld.

In one of the most bizarre twists to this already twisted story, there were, in fact, another set of fighters circling over Washington that morning that *did* have orders to shoot. The Secret Service seems to have done a better job than anyone else in the White House, or in the Pentagon or at NORAD, of keeping up to speed on developments that morning. The Secret Service had its own line to controllers at the FAA, and they took it upon themselves to order the scrambling of fighter jets from the District of Columbia Air National Guard to protect the White House. The commander of this group of fighters, launched from Andrews Air Force Base in Maryland at about 10:40, ordered them to fly "weapons free"—that is, to fire at the will of the lead pilot. The *9/11 Commission Report* states, "The president and the vice president indicated to us they had not been aware that fighters had been scrambled out of Andrews, at the request of the Secret Service and outside the military chain of command. There is no evidence that NORAD headquarters or military officials in the NMCC knew—during the morning of September 11—that the Andrews planes were airborne and operating under different rules of engagement."[43]

As for the fighters from Langley sent up to look for Flight 93, the lack of shoot-down orders was not the only obstacle to their mission. They did not have accurate information about the location of any hijacked plane, nor did they understand the reason they had been scrambled, nor what sort of attack they were facing. They knew they were looking for aircraft but had no idea that the aircraft in question were hijacked commercial airliners full of American civilians. The Langley lead pilot told the 9/11 Commission, "I reverted to the Russian threat. . . . I'm thinking cruise missile threat from the sea. You know you look down and see the Pentagon burning and I thought the bastards snuck one by us. . . . You couldn't see any airplanes, and no one told us anything."[44]

All of this certainly suggests that even if news of the hijackings had been passed on to government leaders sooner than it was, their own failures would still have prevented the military from preventing any of the attacks. The military personnel who were on the spot—the fighter pilots—did not know what kind of target they were looking for, where to look for it, or what to do if they found it. Well after Cheney had informed Rumsfeld that "they've already taken a couple of aircraft out," the pilots were circling over Washington without direction or orders, wondering about phantom Russian cruise missiles.

In fact, the 9/11 Commission took it upon itself to consider what it called a "What If?" scenario: What if the attack by Flight 93 had not been thwarted by its passengers, and the plane had arrived in Washington? The Commission concluded that the fighters would have lacked not only the time, but the information and authorization they needed to stop the attack. In the *9/11*

Report, they write, "NORAD officials have maintained that they would have intercepted and shot down United 93. We are not so sure. We are sure that the nation owes a debt to the passengers of United 93. Their actions saved the lives of countless others, and may have saved either the Capitol or the White House from destruction."[45]

It is difficult, knowing what we know, not to wish that we could trade in the White House and everyone in it for the lives of the passengers on that flight. The events of 9/11 inspired extraordinary courage and resourcefulness in ordinary people facing great risk: flight attendants and passengers aboard doomed airplanes, firefighters and office workers in doomed buildings. In the seats of government power, on the other hand, the events inspired nothing but excuses—and plans for a new war.

Even setting aside what happened in the years and months leading up to 9/11, taking only what happened on the day itself, it is clear that the United States government showed a colossal failure of competence and leadership during an unparalleled national crisis. Yet not one person in the White House—or in the cabinet, or the Pentagon, or anywhere in the Bush administration—was fired because of failure to perform on 9/11. Not one person resigned. With the exception of Richard Clarke, not one person apologized to the victims' families. Nearly twenty-eight hundred people died, and not one of the people responsible for protecting them was held accountable.

3

Why Didn't We Know
What Was Coming?

HOW BUSINESS AS USUAL AT THE FBI AND CIA HELPED
LEAVE THE WAY CLEAR FOR THE 9/11 ATTACKS

On January 15, 2000, two men arrived at Los Angeles International Airport on a United Airlines flight from Bangkok. They had just attended a high-level meeting of Al Qaeda in Kuala Lumpur, Malaysia. The CIA knew of these men; it knew where they had been, and it had their photographs. Though they flew under their own names, the men were not stopped at LAX.

The two men traveled from Los Angeles to San Diego, where they rented an apartment and were listed in the Pacific Bell telephone book. They got themselves Social Security cards, driver's licenses, and credit cards, and bought a Toyota Corolla. They also got season passes to Sea World. And they began attending a local flight school.

The two men received help from a leading member of a local mosque, who was receiving funds from America's ally Saudi Arabia—perhaps directly from the Saudi royal family. With this man's assistance, they moved to a room in the home of a local retired professor. Their new landlord was a paid informant for the FBI's San Diego office.

In August 2001, these two men, now on the East Coast,

logged on to Travelocity.com and bought two tickets on United Flight 77, scheduled to leave Dulles Airport on the morning of September 11, 2001.[1]

In an age of international terrorism, the most powerful defensive weapon is information. This means, in the parlance, "intelligence." In the months and years leading up to 9/11, as the attacks were conceived, planned, and set in motion, the failure to obtain intelligence—and, even more importantly, to use it wisely—left the United States no chance of defending itself.

In today's America, intelligence is provided through a huge, complicated, expensive—and clearly inadequate—network of fifteen separate government agencies, which together make up the U.S. "Intelligence Community." While the numerous military intelligence arms eat up the largest portion of the nation's intelligence budget, the most prominent agencies in the Intelligence Community are the CIA and the FBI.

The Central Intelligence Agency is supposed to gather, analyze, and disseminate foreign intelligence; it is not supposed to operate within the United States, investigate U.S. citizens or legal-resident immigrants, or carry out any enforcement actions other than to "engage in covert action at the president's direction in accordance with applicable law." Until the confirmation of an "intelligence czar" (the director of National Intelligence) in the spring of 2005, the director of Central Intelligence (DCI) remained the top U.S. intelligence post. According to the CIA's own web site, the DCI is "charged . . . with coordinating the nation's intelligence activities and correlating, evaluating and disseminating intelligence which affects national security."

The self-stated mission of the FBI—as revised in the wake of 9/11—is "to protect and defend the United States against terrorist and foreign intelligence threats, to uphold and enforce the criminal laws of the United States, and to provide leadership and criminal justice services to federal, state, municipal, and international agencies and partners." The FBI alone can conduct investigations on American soil, including intelligence gathering on U.S. residents. The Bureau is part of the Department of Justice and answers to the attorney general.

The budgets and personnel figures for the CIA and a number of other agencies are classified. Even the aggregate budget for all intelligence-related activities is declassified only many years after the fact. In 1998, the most recent year for which a figure is available, the aggregate intelligence budget was $26.7 billion. Today it is undoubtedly far higher. In 2003, the budget of the FBI alone was nearly $4.3 billion, and its employees numbered close to thirty thousand.[2]

These two agencies together possessed primary responsibility for preventing the 9/11 attacks. Without the information they were supposed to provide, there was no opportunity for preparation or prevention on the part of law enforcement or the military. There was no effort to tighten security at the borders or in the airports, and military defense of the homeland was left to a handful of fighter jets.

What factors produced an intelligence failure of such stunning proportions? The official critiques have focused on problems in procedural details—the need to reorganize the intelligence bureaucracy, plug loopholes, improve "interagency communications," and remove troublesome restrictions imposed by the Constitution or international law. What these critiques lack is a full assessment of the deep and endemic inadequacies, as well as the politically charged agendas, that left the nation unprepared and unguarded—on 9/11, and today.

WHAT THE CIA DID—AND DIDN'T DO

The story of the CIA's failure to detect Al Qaeda's plans becomes even grimmer in light of its long history of involvement with the terrorist organization. Al Qaeda was a monster that U.S. intelligence helped create.

Osama Bin Laden was one of thousands of young men from throughout the Muslim world who traveled to the Afghan/Pakistani border in the early 1980s to join the mujaheddin in their fight against the Soviet Union, which had invaded Afghanistan in 1979. The CIA was carrying out widespread covert operations in the country, and the Agency actually supported efforts to recruit, train, and arm radical Muslims to fight the Soviets in Afghanistan, working closely with the Pakistani secret service. When the Soviets withdrew from Afghanistan in 1989, the United States abandoned the country to its fate—which included raw poverty, a huge trade in opium, and, before long, the Taliban. It also left behind a large, international force of Islamic extremist guerrillas, willing to die for their cause. It was here that Al Qaeda was born. (This history is discussed in detail in chapter 4.)

In 1991, U.S. troops arrived in the Middle East en masse to fight the Gulf War, and many stayed behind as an occupying force. The idea of U.S. troops settled in on the Arabian Peninsula—with the full cooperation of the Saudi government—enraged Bin Laden beyond anything that had come before. This, combined with ongoing American support for Israel in the Israeli-Palestinian conflict, made the United States the new target of choice for the Al Qaeda fighters armed by the CIA just a few years before.

In addition to being a poor judge of allies, the CIA was a slow learner. It would be many years before they would respond to the threat posed by the organization they had once supported. Shortly after 9/11, the Senate and House Select Committees on Intelligence conducted a joint inquiry into intelligence before and after the attacks. This 2002 report looked back twenty years to the 1983 attacks on the U.S. embassy and a Marine barracks in Beirut, declaring them a "clear warning that terrorist groups were not reluctant to attack U.S. interests."

The first bombing of the World Trade Center in 1993 provided ample evidence that such groups could strike not only U.S. "interests" abroad, but also targets on American soil. As the *Joint Inquiry Report* notes, this attack "led to a growing recognition in the Intelligence Community of a new type of terrorism that did not conform to the Cold War model: violent radical Islamic cells, not linked to any specific country, but united in anti-American zeal."[3]

The CIA proved slow to adjust to this new type of threat, unable to give up the "Cold War model" that had shaped the agency since its inception just after World War II. The creation of a permanent foreign intelligence agency in 1947 had been justified, in large part, by the need to ensure that the United States would never again fall victim to a surprise attack on the order of Pearl Harbor—a fact that takes on a dark irony in the wake of 9/11. But as political scientist Chalmers Johnson notes, from the very beginning, the Agency leadership "saw intelligence analysis as a convenient cover for subversive operations abroad." In Johnson's view, "intelligence collecting and analysis would quickly become camouflage for a private secret army at the personal command of the president devoted to dirty tricks, covert overthrows of foreign governments and planting disinformation—as well as efforts to counter similar operations by the Soviet Union."[4]

The CIA excelled at these covert operations, helping to destabilize governments from Guatemala to Greece and from the Congo to Chile, as well as in Afghanistan (and moving on before they had to deal with the "blowback"—the long-term consequences of their actions). It was far less successful at intelligence gathering, even during the Cold War. Recent histories reveal the Agency as no match for its Soviet counterparts. The CIA lost dozens of its agents and assets behind the Iron Curtain and was unable even to detect the counterespionage operating within its own highest ranks. (In 1994, the chief of counterintelligence for the CIA's Soviet-East Europe division,

Aldrich Ames, was discovered to have been a double agent for ten years.) Spy satellites, which became adept at tracking Soviet arms from the safe distance of space, increasingly took the place of human intelligence.[5]

The terrorist threat that emerged in the early 1990s posed even greater challenges to intelligence gathering and analysis. The United States no longer faced an enemy in the form of a nation-state with an analogous intelligence apparatus—spy vs. spy. Protecting Americans from Al Qaeda meant penetrating the organization's leadership and cells. Bob Graham, a longtime member of the Senate Intelligence Committee, quoted a British intelligence officer who said, "We were able to understand the Soviets from the outside. We are not able to master the capabilities and intentions of the terrorists without getting inside their tents."[6]

The Cold War's state-of-the-art spy satellites were useless against meetings held in desert camps or mountain caves. Whatever communications *were* intercepted could not be translated promptly from Arabic, Dari, or Urdu in a CIA still overloaded with Russian experts. And whatever information *was* secured was unlikely to be shared by an Agency shaped by a culture of secrecy and paranoia.

On-the-ground human resources were a still bigger problem. Even after the first World Trade Center bombing, it took nearly three years, until January 1996, for the CIA to create a unit dedicated to collecting intelligence on Al Qaeda and its links to other armed Islamic militant groups. This unit operated as part of the Agency's Counterterrorist Center (CTC), which had been established ten years earlier, in 1986.[7]

These dedicated units never succeeded in "getting inside the tents" of the terrorists. "CIA had no penetration of Al Qaeda's leadership and never obtained intelligence that was sufficient for action against Usama Bin Laden from anyone," the Joint Inquiry concluded.[8] This despite the fact that John Walker Lindh and seven other Americans volunteers in their twenties successfully joined Al Qaeda with seeming ease, and took training in the group's camps in Afghanistan. James Bamford, in his book *A Pretext for War* points out that Lindh was in Afghanistan when Bin Laden, accompanied by Egyptian Islamic Jihad leader Ayman al-Zawahiri, announced the merger of Al Qaeda and the Egyptian group. Lindh learned of Bin Laden's plans, including the dispatch of some fifty terrorists to carry out suicide attacks against the United States and Israel. He later told investigators that the four flights hijacked on 9/11 were supposed to have been five, with the fifth plane crashing into the White House. (The pilot of that plane was not able to get a visa.) Another American Al Qaeda volunteer had a private interview with Bin Laden.[9] If these Americans successfully "penetrated" Al Qaeda leadership and had no trouble finding out about their plans, why were the adroit spies of the CIA never able to do the same?

The U.S. Intelligence Community's inability to place its own spies within Al Qaeda's ranks meant that they had to get all of their information second-, third-, and fourth-hand, from various informants—some of them paid, some politically motivated—and foreign intelligence agencies, all of which had agendas of their own. "Lacking access to senior, high level al-Qa'ida leadership, the [Intelligence] Community relied on secondhand, fragmented and often questionable human intelligence information, a great deal of which was obtained from volunteers or sources obtained through the efforts of foreign liaison," the Joint Inquiry concludes.[10]

America's prime ally in the region, Saudi Arabia, should have been a valuable resource for intelligence gathering. This was the homeland of Bin Laden and many Al Qaeda members, including fifteen of the nineteen 9/11 hijackers. It was the source of a huge portion of Al Qaeda's funding. The Joint Inquiry's discussion of the Saudis role in pre-9/11 intelligence is one of the most heavily redacted sections in its report. The remaining fragments of testimony are telling. "The Committees heard testimony from U.S. Government personnel that Saudi officials had been uncooperative and often did not act on information implicating Saudi nationals." One official said, "it was clear from 1996 that the Saudi Government would not cooperate with the United States on matters relating to Usama Bin Laden." Another "cited greater Saudi cooperation when asked how the September 11 attacks might have been prevented."[11]

Another American ally in the region, Pakistan, was also worse than useless as a resource for U.S. intelligence. The CIA's Pakistani counterpart, the ISI, was a strong supporter of the Taliban and often also supported Al Qaeda. (For more on the Pakistani and Saudi connections, see chapter 4.)

In August 1996 Bin Laden issued a fatwa authorizing attacks on Western interests on the Arabian Peninsula. Two years later, in February 1998, he issued a second fatwa, this time declaring, "The ruling to kill Americans and their allies—civilians and military—is an individual duty for every Muslim who can do it in any country in which it is possible."[12]

But it took the August 1998 bombings of the American embassies in Kenya and Tanzania, which killed 220 people and could be traced directly to Bin Laden, to really bring Al Qaeda to the center of the CIA's attention. Even at this point, Chalmers Johnson writes, "the CIA and the White House awoke to the Islamist threat, but they defined it almost exclusively in terms of Osama bin Laden's leadership of al-Qaida and failed to see the larger context. They did not target the Taliban, Pakistani military intelligence, or the funds flowing to the Taliban and al-Qaida from Saudi Arabia and the United Arab Emirates. Instead, they devoted themselves to trying to capture or kill bin Laden."[13]

Indeed, the August 20 bombing campaign ordered by President Clinton in response to the embassy attacks was widely considered a failure because it did not kill Bin Laden, although it destroyed some Al Qaeda sites. Subsequent attacks were considered, but the CIA, dependent upon a handful of questionable Afghan assets, failed to locate Bin Laden's position with enough advance notice. According to the Joint Inquiry, "senior U.S. military officials were reluctant to use U.S. military assets to conduct offensive counterterrorism efforts in Afghanistan directed against al-Qa'ida prior to September 11. At least in part this reluctance was driven by the military's view that the Intelligence Community was unable to provide the intelligence needed to support military operations."[14] (For a discussion of possible Pakistani and Saudi roles in the failure of these attacks, see chapter 4.)

There were political factors as well. Clinton, who was deep in the Monica Lewinsky scandal, decided not to undertake actions with a high risk of failure, or to attack Afghanistan on a larger scale. The August bombings, which took place three days after Clinton's interrogation about his sex life, had been widely criticized as a crass attempt to draw attention away from Monicagate. And while Clinton apparently took the threat of Al Qaeda seriously, he was also destined to take into account his already beleaguered political career.

However, according to several press reports, as well as testimony by former National Security Advisor Sandy Berger, the CIA had clear authorization to use lethal force against Bin Laden, who was considered fair game in the cause of self-defense. Yet he stayed alive and well throughout the remainder of the Clinton administration. Richard Clarke writes, "Some have claimed that the lethal authorizations were convoluted and the 'people in the field' did not know what they could do. . . . I believe that those in CIA who claim the authorizations were insufficient or unclear are throwing up that claim as an excuse to cover the fact that they were pathetically unable to accomplish the mission."[15]

In late 1999 there was news of another attempted attack aimed at the Los Angeles International Airport, which was foiled when the attacker was stopped crossing the Canadian border. A second apparent millennium plot was detected and stopped in Jordan. In October 2000, on the eve of the Bush-Gore presidential election, the bombing of the destroyer USS *Cole*, docked in Aden, Yemen, killed seventeen sailors. Several months would pass before the CIA agreed to attribute the attack to Al Qaeda, and in the waning days of the Clinton presidency, no action was taken.[16]

WHAT THE WHITE HOUSE DID—AND DIDN'T DO

Any analysis of intelligence failures in the crucial months leading up to 9/11 must take into account the influence of political will. Thirty years ago, in the course of a scathing report on CIA covert actions, Congress's Pike Committee denounced the idea that such actions could be attributed to the "rogue" nature of intelligence agencies. "All evidence in hand suggests that the CIA, far from being out of control, has been utterly responsive to the instructions of the president and the assistant to the president for National Security Affairs," the report concluded.[17] The Pike Committee was referring to Richard Nixon and Henry Kissinger, but they could just as well have been describing Bush and Cheney and Condoleeza Rice.

Five days after George W. Bush was sworn in, Richard Clarke sent a memo to Condoleeza Rice, Bush's new National Security Advisor, urging that the new administration make the threat of Al Qaeda a top priority, and requesting an immediate top-level meeting on the subject. Clarke's memo began, "As we noted in our briefings for you, *al Qida* is not some narrow, little terrorist issue that needs to be included in broader regional policy. Rather, several of our regional policies need to address centrally the transnational challenge to the US and our interests posed by the *al Qida* network." Attached to that memo was a "year-end 2000 strategy on Al Qaeda developed by the last administration to give to you," entitled "Strategy for Eliminating the Threat from the Jihadist Networks of al Qida: Status and Prospects."

Among other things, this memo said Al Qaeda was trying to obtain weapons of mass destruction, and blamed Al Qaeda for the attack on the USS *Cole*. Turning to the situation within the United States, Clarke wrote, "Al Qaeda is present in the United States. Al Qaeda has been linked to terrorist operations in the U.S., while also conducting recruiting and fundraising activities. U.S. citizens have also been linked to Al Qaeda." The memo continued, "A suspect in the East Africa bombings (former US Army Sergeant Ali Muhammad) has informed [name redacted] that an extensive network of Al Qaeda 'sleeper' agents currently exists in the U.S."[18] Another detailed assessment of terrorism threats was released during Bush's first weeks in office. The U.S. Commission on National Security/21st Century—known as the Hart-Rudman Commission—had been convened in 1998 to make broad recommendations for U.S. security in the new millennium. The Commission's report, released on January 31, 2001, concluded that "the combination of unconventional weapons proliferation with the persistence of international terrorism will end the relative invulnerability of the U.S. homeland to catastrophic attack," and predicted that a major attack on U.S. soil was likely to take place in the future.[19]

What happened—or did not happen—in the subsequent eight months? How could the nation have been so unprepared for the 9/11 attacks? The false and facile explanations that arose in the days following the September 11 attacks were summed up by Bob Graham in his 2004 book *Intelligence Matters*. The former senator from Florida, generally considered a conservative Democrat who is hawkish on intelligence, served for ten years on the Senate Intelligence Committee and co-chaired the 2002 Congressional Joint Inquiry into intelligence failures before the 9/11 attacks. (Despite extensive redaction and a lack of cooperative

Bush administration sources, this report was generally more rigorous than the 9/11 Commission's report—and Graham's own book goes further still.)

Shortly after 9/11, Graham writes, "a number of things were being said about the attacks. The first was that it was a surprise, a bolt from the blue. The second was that no one could have imagined such an attack carried out in such a manner. The third, that since no one could have envisaged the use of commercial aircraft as a weapon of mass destruction, no one could be held accountable. The fourth was that for all the devastation, the attack was basically quite simple." Graham notes that while all of these statements quickly became "truisms," they were also all wrong.[20]

In fact, the Congressional Joint Inquiry found that "Beginning in 1998 and continuing into the summer of 2001, the Intelligence Community received a modest, but relatively steady stream of intelligence reporting that indicated the possibility of terrorist attacks within the United States." These warning signs were clear, credible, and cumulative.

By the middle of 2001, the CIA's Bin Laden unit had grown from sixteen to forty members and "had unprecedented access to senior agency officials and White House policymakers." The report also notes that "during the spring and summer of 2001, the Intelligence Community experienced a significant increase in information indicating that Bin Laden and al-Qa'ida intended to strike against U.S. interests in the very near future."[21]

The National Security Agency, through its vast surveillance network, reported "at least 33 communications indicating a possible, imminent terrorist attack in 2001. Senior U.S. Government officials were advised by the Intelligence Community on June 28 and July 10, 2001, that the attacks were expected, among other things, to 'have dramatic consequences on governments or cause major casualties' and that 'attack preparations have been made. Attack will occur with little or no warning.'"[22]

Many of these "threat-specific warnings," the Joint Inquiry concluded, reached the office of the president. "In August 2001, a closely held intelligence report included information that Bin Laden had wanted to conduct attacks in the United States since 1997."[23] This was the infamous Presidential Daily Briefing, or PDB, the title of which—"Bin Laden Determined to Strike in U.S."—Condoleeza Rice would be so reluctant to state publicly before the 9/11 Commission. Rice would also describe the briefing as containing an "historical perspective" on Bin Laden's methods. And the administration would resist releasing its contents to the public or even to the Congress.

A reading of the brief shows why the White House wanted it to remain secret. In a statement italicized by its authors for emphasis, the briefing declared that Al Qaeda members "*have resided in or traveled to the US for years, and the group apparently maintains a support structure that could aid attacks.*" Later, the report noted that FBI information collected since 1998 "indicates patterns of suspicious activity in this country consistent with preparations for hijackings and or other types of attacks, including recent surveillance of federal buildings in New York."[24]

Not only was the Intelligence Community fully aware of the growing danger of an attack, it also had indications such attacks might well involve planes as weapons. The Joint Inquiry report summarized, "From at least 1994, and continuing into the summer of 2001, the Intelligence Community received information indicating that terrorists were contemplating, among other means of attack, the use of aircraft as weapons." For example, intelligence agencies "received information in 1998 about a Bin Laden operation that would involve flying an explosive laden aircraft into a U.S. airport and, in summer 2001, about a plot to bomb a U.S. embassy from an airplane or crash an airplane into it. The FBI and CIA were also aware that convicted terrorist Abdul Hakim Murad and several others had discussed the possibility of crashing an airplane into CIA headquarters as part of 'the Bojinka Plot' in the Philippines."[25] (The Bojinka Plot, which aimed to simultaneously hijack and crash a dozen aircraft into landmarks worldwide, is described in chapter 1.)

Bob Graham tallies up the information received in the spring and summer of 2001, and finds no fewer than "twelve instances in which we had learned of terrorist plans to use airplanes as weapons."[26] Paul Thompson and the Center for Cooperative Research, in compiling their *Terror Timeline*, found even more. Numerous reports of pre-9/11 threats of an imminent attack on America using planes were quickly uncovered by the international press in the days and months following the attacks. Following are some examples.

In 1999, British intelligence gave a secret report to the U.S. embassy stating that Al Qaeda had plans to use "commercial aircraft in unconventional ways possibly as flying bombs," according to a June 9, 2002, report in the Sunday *Times* of London. And in July and August 2001, according to British news sources, the Brits sent two more warnings, the second of which specifically told the U.S. to expect multiple airline hijackings by Al Qaeda.

In June 2001, German intelligence warned the United States, Britain, and Israel that Middle Eastern terrorists were planning to hijack commercial aircraft and use them as weapons to attack "American and Israeli symbols which stand out." These warnings were reported in the September 13, 2001, *Frankfurter Allgemeine Zeitung*.

In late July 2001, Egyptian intelligence received a report from an undercover agent in Afghanistan that "20 al Qaeda members had slipped into the U.S., and four of them had received flight training on Cessnas. To the Egyptians, pilots of small planes didn't sound terribly alarming, but they passed on the message to the CIA anyway, fully expecting Washington to request information. The request never came," according to a CBS News story of October 9, 2002.

In late summer 2001, Jordanian intelligence intercepted a message stating that a major attack was being planned inside the United States and that aircraft would be used. The code name of the operation, they said, was the Big Wedding, which did in fact turn out to be the code name of the 9/11 plot. The message was passed to U.S. intelligence through several channels. This nugget was reported in the May 21, 2002, *International Herald Tribune*.

Russian president Vladimir Putin publicly stated that he ordered his intelligence agencies to alert the United States in the summer of 2001 that suicide pilots were training for attacks on U.S. targets, according to a Fox News story on May 17, 2002. Just five days after the 9/11 attacks, Agence France-Presse reported that the head of Russian intelligence said of the alerts given to the U.S., "We had clearly warned them" on several occasions, but they "did not pay the necessary attention."

Five days before 9/11, a priest named Jean-Marie Benjamin was told by a Muslim at an Italian wedding of a plot to attack the United States and Britain, using hijacked airplanes as weapons. He wasn't told the specifics of time or place, but he immediately passed what he knew on to a judge and several politicians in Italy. Presumably this Muslim confided in him because Benjamin has done considerable charity work in Muslim countries and is considered "one of the West's most knowledgeable experts on the Muslim world," according to a September 16, 2001, article by the Italian news service zenit.org. This information may have come from the Milan Al Qaeda cell, which forged documents for the organization's operations. Wiretaps indicated that its members were aware of a plot very much like 9/11—a year before the attacks. For instance, in August 2000, one terrorist in Milan was recorded as saying to another, "I'm studying airplanes. I hope, God willing, that I can bring you a window or a piece of an airplane the next time we see each other." The comment was followed by laughter, according to a *Los Angeles Times* account on May 29, 2002. In January 2001, a terrorist asked if certain forged documents were for "the brothers going to the United States"— and was angrily rebuked by another, who told him not to talk about that "very, very secret" plan. In March 2001, the Italian government gave the U.S. a warning based on these wiretaps, Fox News reported on May 17, 2002.[27]

There is even substantial evidence that the United States took steps to prepare for an attack similar to the 9/11 attacks at the July 2001 G8 economic summit in Genoa, Italy. Egyptian intelligence services reportedly informed U.S. intelligence that it had clues that Al Qaeda might be planning to attack Bush and other leaders using "planes stuffed with explosives." In fact, as part of the huge security effort mounted for the summit, Italy closed the airspace above Genoa during the summit and installed anti-aircraft missiles. Two days before the summit began, the BBC reported, "The huge force of officers and equipment which has been assembled to deal with unrest has been spurred on by a warning that supporters of Saudi dissident Osama bin Laden might attempt an air attack on some of the world leaders present."[28] Bush himself would choose to stay on an offshore aircraft carrier, rather than in Genoa.

Clearly, serious problems arose from what the 9/11 Commission would rather euphemistically call "poor inter-agency communication." Many of these explosive facts, gathered by various sources—the NSA as well as the CIA and FBI—never found their way into the hands of the people who needed them most. For instance, the chief of the Radical Fundamentalist Unit in the FBI's Counterterrorism Division told the Joint Inquiry that he was completely unaware of any reports of Al Qaeda planning this kind of attack within the United States.

But it is equally clear that in the critical months leading up to 9/11, intelligence services were responding to the priorities set for them by the Bush administration—and that these priorities were shaped by a clear political agenda.

The 2002 Joint Inquiry report states, "The Joint Inquiry heard repeatedly about intelligence priorities that competed contemporaneously with Bin Laden for personnel and funds. These included a range of regional and global issues."[29]

Richard Clarke, among others, has been more explicit in identifying these competing priorities, especially as concerned the new Bush administration. Dick Cheney, according to Clarke, frequently visited CIA headquarters in Langley, but "most of the visits focused on Iraq and left midlevel managers and analysts wondering whether the seasoned Vice President was right about the Iraqi threat; perhaps they should adjust their own analysis."[30] In May 2001, Bush would put Cheney in charge of an initiative to examine "national preparedness" in general, and especially preparation for "managing a possible attack by weapons of mass destruction." According to the *9/11 Commission Report*, "The next few months were mainly spent organizing the effort and bringing an admiral from the Sixth Fleet back to Washington to manage it. The vice president's task force was just getting underway when the 9/11 attack occurred."[31]

Clarke describes the first high-level meeting on Al Qaeda, which did not take place until April 2001. In the meeting, according to Clarke, then Deputy Secretary of Defense Paul Wolfowitz expressed doubt that Al Qaeda could have mounted such attacks as the 1993 World Trade Center bombing without a state sponsor, and argued that the administration should also be looking at "Iraqi terrorism." The CIA deputy director present, according to Clarke, said, "We have no evidence of any active Iraqi terrorist threat against the U.S." A top-level "Principals Committee" meeting on Al Qaeda did not take place until September 4, 2001. There, Clarke says, Wolfowitz's boss Donald Rumsfeld took a similar position, insisting that attention be paid to other sources of terrorism, such as Iraq.[32] (In Clarke's view, National Security Advisor Condoleeza Rice took the Al Qaeda threat more seriously, but was a consummate team player who would not question the agenda set by Rumsfeld, Cheney, and Bush.) By this time, of course, Rumsfeld, Cheney, and others were also well into planning a possible 2002 invasion of Iraq. Apparently, their efforts to connect Iraq to terrorism—presumably as a potential justification for such an invasion—began not after, but before the 9/11 attacks.

Defending his position that the crucial August 6 PDB had contained "no actionable intelligence," Bush said, "There was not a time and place of an attack. It said Osama Bin Laden had designs on America. Well, I knew that. What I wanted to know was, is there anything specifically going to take place in America that we needed to react to?"[33] Bob Graham writes that Bush's statement "revealed a stunning lack of understanding about how both intelligence and leadership work. . . . We all wish intelligence could tell us exactly what is going to happen, when, and where. But really what intelligence can do is present an accurate picture of the threats, targets, and methods. It is incumbent on the consumer of intelligence, be it a Congressional staffer or the president, to make policy judgments and recommendations based on that intelligence."[34]

The August 6 brief represented the best information the Intelligence Community could muster; it communicated directly to the president Al Qaeda's intention to attack, its preparation for hijackings, and its surveillance of buildings in New York. It did not name dates, times, or places, but nothing in the report denied that the attacks might well be imminent.

Yet no action was taken by the White House as a result of this briefing. And, as Graham documents, in a departure from usual procedures, its key paragraphs were not included in that day's Senior Intelligence Executive Brief, or SEIB, which circulates to about three hundred people, including the House and Senate

Intelligence Committees, senior personnel in defense and intelligence, and the FAA.

It is possible that other factors, in addition to its obsession with Iraq, influenced the Bush administration's lack of action in response to the PDB and other warnings. Bob Graham notes the "administration's lack of curiosity" about the briefing's report of a U.S.-based "support structure that could aid attacks" by the terrorist network. Graham suggests that an aggressive pursuit of these "support structures" would likely lead to Bush's special friends the Saudis.[35] (The Saudi money trail is discussed in detail in chapter 4.)

Whether by negligence or intention, the White House failed to "connect the dots" provided by intelligence in the months leading up to 9/11. Clearly, had the CIA been more effective—less attached to a stale Cold War model or to swashbuckling covert ops, more successful at penetrating Al Qaeda and at collecting, translating, and analyzing intelligence, less secretive and territorial about their work—the White House leadership would have received more and clearer intelligence on the impending attacks. However, reviewing the Bush administration's lack of response to the information it did receive, it is far from clear that better intelligence would have made much difference.

In the aftermath of the attacks, however, the Intelligence Community has absorbed any blame while at the same time aided in a cover-up. Both FBI directors, Louis Freeh and Robert Mueller, have been models of slick obfuscation in their testimony before the Joint Inquiry and the 9/11 Commission. (See chapter 5.) Mueller remains at the head of an increasingly powerful and well-funded FBI. Freeh (who looks particularly bad in after-the-fact assessments) has secured an appointment as counsel at MBNA, one of the nation's largest credit card issuers and also one of the largest donors to George W. Bush's campaigns. George Tenet proved a bit less untouchable than his FBI counterparts but performed well enough under fire to earn the Presidential Medal of Freedom after his well-timed resignation. The ever-loyal Condi Rice, who took the brief gust of heat from the 9/11 Commission on the ignored PDB, was, of course, promoted to secretary of state. And Bush, Cheney, and Rumsfeld parlayed their "failure" into a long-desired war against Iraq, as well as a second term.

Any doubts about the Intelligence Community's willingness to fall on its sword for the president should be laid to rest after witnessing its conduct on Iraq's nonexistent WMDs. Any doubts about the Bush administration's respect for its intelligence services should be laid to rest by its attitude toward the exposure of an undercover operative, Valerie Plame, in a political vendetta.

WHAT THE FBI DID—AND DIDN'T DO

The year prior to the 9/11 attacks found a number of future hijackers, as well as the mastermind of the attacks, on American soil, on the turf of the FBI. While the Bureau was handicapped, in a few cases, by a lack of information flow from the CIA, the FBI showed itself more than capable of missing, ignoring, or burying vital clues that might have thwarted the attacks.

The problems began at the top, in the priorities set by FBI leadership and especially by Attorney General John Ashcroft. Several accounts show Ashcroft as remarkably uninterested in terrorism in the months leading up to the 9/11 attacks. A harsh view of Ashcroft's priorities was contained in the 9/11 Commission testimony of Thomas Pickard, who served as acting director of the FBI from June 25 to September 4, 2001, in the critical months between the resignation of Louis Freeh and the appointment of Robert Mueller. Pickard (who had been considered a strong Bush ally) testified that after he brought the rising threat of Al Qaeda to Ashcroft's attention several times, the attorney general rejected any further briefings on the subject. Ashcroft also

denied an August 2001 plea for an additional $58 million to com-
bat Al Qaeda; the rejection came through on September 10.

On May 10, 2001, Ashcroft issued a memo outlining the
strategic goals of the Justice Department; it made no mention of
counterterrorism. Dale Watson, then the FBI's assistant director
for counterterrorism and counterintelligence, told the 9/11 Commission that he "almost fell out of [his] chair" when he read
Ashcroft's memo.

In his own testimony, Ashcroft insisted he believed any attacks
would take place abroad, outside of his purview. In the words of
the *Washington Post*, he also "sought to blame the Clinton administration for many of the shortcomings in counterterrorism strate-
gies before the attacks, taking the unusual step of publicly citing
the work of a Democratic member of the commission, Jamie S.
Gorelick, who served as a deputy attorney general in the Clinton
administration. Ashcroft announced the declassification and
release of a 1995 memo she wrote that outlined legal rules on sharing intelligence information, characterizing the guidelines as 'the
single greatest structural cause for the September 11th problem.'"[36]

Ashcroft may have prepared this line of defense in response to
what he knew was coming. According to the *New York Times*, the
Justice Department had seen a draft report, prepared by the 9/11
Commission staff, in the days immediately prior to the set of public hearings where Ashcroft, Pickard, and others would testify.
"Commission officials" told the *Times* that the Justice Department
had "mounted an aggressive effort to persuade the commission to
rewrite parts of report dealing with Ashcroft." The final *9/11 Commission Report* contains just over one page on Ashcroft's leadership.
It does mention the May memo, but omits many other issues
raised in the draft—including the fact that Ashcroft had made the
decision, in the summer of 2001, to begin traveling exclusively by
government jet, rather than on commercial airliners.[37]

There were problems on the ground as well as at the top. Many of these had roots in the historic nature of the Bureau, which left the rank-and-file of the FBI unprepared to deal with the challenges posed by Al Qaeda.

A truism that emerged after 9/11 is that the FBI was simply a federal police force, not set up or authorized to do domestic intelligence. The history of the Bureau clearly tells another story. During J. Edgar Hoover's reign (1924–72), a primary mission of the FBI was to gather intelligence on any persons or group Hoover deemed "subversive." These operations reached their height during the McCarthy era and then simply moved deeper underground. The secret COINTELPRO (Counterintelligence Program), launched in 1956, aimed to spy on and disrupt such "enemies of the American way of life" as civil rights, antiwar, student, and even women's liberation groups, as well as the John Birch Society and the Ku Klux Klan. Under this program, the FBI conducted half a million investigations of so-called subversives and maintained files on well over a million Americans. They tapped phones, opened mail, planted bugs, and burglarized homes and offices. At least twenty-six thousand individuals were at one point catalogued on an FBI list of persons to be rounded up in the event of a "national emergency."[38]

After Hoover died and the worst excesses of COINTELPRO were exposed by congressional investigations in the 1970s, these types of operations were toned down, but never eliminated. In their book *Terrorism and the Constitution*, David Cole and James X. Dempsey document FBI intelligence investigations of Amnesty International, of CISPES (Committee in Solidarity with the People of El Salvador), and other groups opposing the Reagan administration's policies in Central America, of the environmental group Earth First!, the gay rights group ACT UP, and several Arab-American and pro-Palestinian organizations.[39]

In carrying out these operations, the FBI used classic intelligence-gathering methods—not only conducting electronic surveillance and maintaining extensive files on suspects and their contacts, but also penetrating groups by placing undercover agents in their midst or recruiting informants. This is precisely the sort of work that was so conspicuously absent from intelligence activities aimed at Al Qaeda in the years and months leading up to 9/11. If the FBI could collect this kind of information on nonviolent political activists, how could it fail so completely when faced with cells of violent jihadists, planning a major attack on American soil?

The FBI was attached to its way of doing things, and the infrastructure and communications at the fittingly named Bureau made the CIA look like a model of efficiency. But the FBI's problems were political as well as procedural. Like the CIA, the FBI's domestic intelligence program was built on a Cold War model, which persisted long after the end of the Cold War. In particular, it was shaped by the towering figure of Hoover, who was obsessed with the Red Menace (and a confirmed racist to boot). Over the years, the FBI had absorbed what attorney and intelligence historian Frank Donner called a "culture of countersubversion." Its program of domestic surveillance and penetration rarely targeted genuine threats to public safety, and almost never led to arrests or prosecutions. (COINTELPRO's half-million investigations never resulted in a single conviction.) Instead, it was designed to monitor and suppress domestic dissent, especially from the Left.[40]

While it focused its domestic intelligence on progressive peace and social justice groups whose activities were nonviolent (and seldom even illegal), the FBI had virtually no accountability; since it faced no real threat, there was no way it could fail. But when faced with the racist Far Right of the 1980s and 1990s—a political movement that presented a genuine terrorist threat—the FBI was ineffective, unable to foil even a major attack that destroyed its own headquarters in the Oklahoma City Federal Building in

1995.[41] And when faced with foreign terrorists planning an even more devastating attack, the Bureau was in far over its head.

The congressional *Joint Inquiry Report* documents the state of affairs at the pre-9/11 FBI—somewhat more effectively than the later *9/11 Commission Report.* Testimony by whistle-blowers goes further.

The FBI formed a Radical Fundamentalist Unit in 1994, a Counterterrorism Center in 1996, and a dedicated Usama Bin Ladin Unit in 1999. It also expanded its stationing of agents abroad as legal attachés, or "legats," to arrest terrorists outside of the United States.[42] During the Clinton years, according to NSA Sandy Berger, the "FBI's counterterrorism staff budget increased by 250% and their counterterrorism budget increased by nearly 350%."[43] But these investments seemed to have produced little more than the illusion of a response to the growing threat.

Richard Clarke told the Joint Inquiry that in 2000 "it became very clear to the [FBI] Assistant Director for Counterterrorism [that] there was the potential for sleeper cells in the United States"; he initiated efforts to bring the Bureau's fifty-six field offices up to speed. But when Clarke visited a handful of these offices, "I got sort of blank looks of 'what is al-Qa'ida?'"[44]

It is hardly surprising that information was slow to trickle down from the top or move among various offices and divisions. Communications systems at the Bureau were a bureaucratic travesty and an operational disaster. The Bureau that had once maintained files on a million peaceful American activists did not move its paper case files and indices onto computers until the astonishingly late date of 1995. Their "Automated Case System" was, according to the Joint Inquiry, "unfriendly, unreliable and unworkable." Many agents simply did not use it, either to research or to log cases. (In September 2002, a year after the attacks, the *Joint Inquiry Report* showed "68,000 outstanding leads directed to the Counterterrorism Division, dating back to 1995."[45])

While J. Edgar Hoover had maintained hundreds of agents trained to pursue the Red Menace, the FBI had a dearth of agents who understood Islamic fundamentalism or even Middle Eastern cultures. Fewer than two dozen agents spoke Arabic. Any intelligence the Bureau managed to acquire was likely to be lost in translation. Prior to September 11, the intelligence services as a whole had "backlogs in materials awaiting translation, a shortage of language specialists and language-qualified field officers, and a readiness level of only 30% in the most critical terrorism-related languages."[46]

The case of Sibel Edmonds, a young Turkish-American woman who worked as a translator in the FBI's Washington, D.C., field office in the fevered days following the 9/11 attacks, provides a disquieting snapshot of the Bureau's language translation section at work. She reported intentional slowdowns designed to increase the translation budget; other translators assigned to work in languages they did not speak; numerous security breaches; and an environment characterized by petty competition and rampant paranoia. When she raised questions about all of these things, she was first harassed and then fired. Edmonds's public battle against her treatment and the subsequent cover-up have inspired a host of similar accounts from other FBI whistle-blowers. (For more on Sibel Edmonds, see chapter 5.[47])

A similar environment apparently existed for the skilled analysts who were assigned to counterterrorism under the budget windfalls of the 1990s. The Joint Inquiry found that, "In 1996, the FBI hired approximately fifty strategic analysts for counterterrorism purposes, many with advanced degrees. According to both current and former FBI analytic personnel and supervisors, most of those analysts left the Bureau within two years because they were dissatisfied with the role of strategic analysis at the FBI." By September 11, 2001, only one strategic analyst was assigned to Al Qaeda, along with ten tactical analysts. Shortly after the attacks, in January 2002, an internal FBI study "found that 66% of the FBI's 1200 'Intelligence Research Specialists' (Strategic Analysts) were unqualified" and that "newly assigned strategic and operational analysts received little counterterrorism training upon assuming their positions."[48]

"Analysis" is no mysterious process. It means, in what is now the popular parlance, "connecting the dots" provided by raw data. For example, according to the Joint Inquiry, the mastermind of the 9/11 attacks was Khalid Sheikh Mohammed. "The information indicates that KSM presented a plan to Osama Bin Laden to mount an attack using small rental aircraft filled with explosives. Osama Bin Laden reportedly suggested using even larger planes. Thus, the idea of hijacking commercial airliners took hold. Thereafter, KSM reportedly instructed and trained the hijackers for their mission, including directing them to undergo pilot training." The Intelligence Community had no shortage of information on Khalid Sheikh Mohammed, who had been linked to the Bojinka Plot in 1995, and later to the first World Trade Center bombing, and was indicted by a New York grand jury in 1996. Yet there was no reaction when, in June 2001, a report was circulated to intelligence agencies stating that "KSM" had himself traveled recently to the United States and was recruiting others to do so, telling them he could arrange their entry. "The clear implication of his comments," according to the *Joint Inquiry Report*, "was that they would be engaged in planning terrorist-related activities. Although this particular report was sent from the CIA to the FBI, neither agency apparently recognized the significance of a Bin Laden lieutenant sending terrorists to the United States and asking them to establish contacts with colleagues already there." The CIA's Counterterrorism Center, in fact, commented, "We doubt the real [KSM] would do this" because he would not be so bold as to give the CIA "an opportunity to pick him up."[49]

Many of the future hijackers took their flight training on

American soil. Several came to the attention of alert rank-and-file agents in FBI field offices, who tried in vain to pass the information on. In the now widely known case of the "Phoenix Memo," an agent in the Phoenix field office noticed an "inordinate number of individuals of investigative interest" taking training in civil aviation in Arizona, and explicitly raised the possibility of a connection to Al Qaeda and a future terrorist action. In July 2001, he communicated his concerns and his request for further investigation to eight people in the Radical Fundamentalist Unit, the Usama Bin Ladin Unit, and the international terrorism squad in New York. Only three of the recipients recalled reading the memo; none took any action. At least two of the individuals identified in the Phoenix Memo were indeed tied to Al Qaeda; one, a trained pilot, was an associate of future Flight 77 hijacker Hani Hanjour, possibly sent to evaluate Hanjour's flying skills before the attacks were set in motion.[50]

In a still more famous case, Zacarias Moussaoui was reported to the FBI's Minneapolis office after he tried to register for flight training. Moussaoui was detained on a visa violation on August 16, 2001. FBI headquarters (erroneously) told Minneapolis that they could not get a search warrant for Moussaoui's belongings, which were later shown to contain clues to the attack. Much has been made of this error, which is often blamed on excessive concern for civil liberties. Less is made of the intelligence leadership's failure to act upon the substantial information the Minneapolis office *did* provide. Based upon their interviews with Moussaoui, Minneapolis quickly sent detailed information to the Bureau's Radical Fundamentalist Unit (RFU) and the CIA's Counterterrorism Center (CTC). This information raised suspicions that Moussaoui and his roommate might be "suspect 747 airline attackers" and "suspect airline suicide attackers" who could be "involved in a larger plot to target airlines traveling from Europe to the U.S." A week later, the CTC passed on this information to

CIA stations abroad. Another week later, on September 4, the RFU sent a less explicit version to others in the Intelligence Community and to other government agencies, including the FAA. Nothing happened.[51]

Most stunning of all is the story of the two Flight 77 hijackers who came in contact with U.S. intelligence services repeatedly, both before and during their stay in the United States. The story begins with an NSA (National Security Agency) wiretap of a known Al Qaeda safe house in Yemen, which told American intelligence that Al Qaeda operatives would have a key strategy meeting in early January 2000 in Kuala Lumpur. Among these operatives, the call indicated, was an Al Qaeda veteran named Khalid Al Mihdhar, a Saudi who had fought for Al Qaeda in Bosnia and Chechnya and trained in Bin Laden's Afghan camps. The CIA put him under surveillance and, at a stopover in the United Arab Emirates on the way to Malaysia, detained him long enough to make a copy of his passport. When Al Mihdhar landed in Kuala Lumpur, however, the CIA left it to the Malaysian Security Service to run surveillance.

In Kuala Lumpur Al Mihdhar met other Al Qaeda members, including Nawaf Al Hazmi, another Saudi national with battle experience in Bosnia, Chechnya, and Afghanistan. Although the CIA was well aware of the importance of this meeting, neither the Agency nor Malaysian Security attempted to bug the meeting. But on January 8, Malaysian Security told the CIA it had observed three men from the conference, including Al Mihdhar and Al Hazmi, take a plane for Bangkok. By the time CIA agents arrived in the Bangkok airport, the plane had gone and the men had disappeared.[52]

A few days later, Al Mihdhar and Al Hazmi—two known Al Qaeda operatives destined to participate in the 9/11 attacks— openly took a United Airlines flight from Bangkok to Los Angeles, where they were admitted without comment. By that time, according the *Joint Inquiry Report*, "The CIA and NSA had sufficient information available concerning future hijackers al-Mihdhar and al-Hamzi to connect them to Usama Bin Ladin, the East Africa embassy bombings, and the USS *Cole* attack . . . and there were at least three different occasions when these individuals should have been placed on the State Department's TIPOFF watchlist and the INS and Customs watchlists."[53]

Only in July 2001 did a few analysts, acting on their own initiative, confirm that both men had entered the United States. They notified the State Department and FBI headquarters—which told its field office in New York, but not its offices in Los Angeles or San Diego, to search for the two. And no one thought to tell the FAA, INS, or Customs service not to let these men fly on planes.[54]

Once the two future hijackers entered the United States, the FBI joined the CIA in allowing them to pass under their noses. Al Mihdhar and Al Hazmi traveled from Los Angeles to San Diego and rented an apartment; they obtained Social Security cards, driver's licenses, credit cards, and a car; and they began their flight training.

The two men had contact with a Soviet diplomat who was also a radical imam at a Los Angeles mosque that had come to the attention of the FBI. They had repeated contact with a leader of the local Saudi community, who had also made his way into the FBI's files; he would later be exposed as a possible conduit for Saudi funding to the hijackers. (See chapter 4 for details.)

Finally, they had extensive contact with an FBI informant—in fact, they lived in his home. Partway into their stay in San Diego, Al Mihdhar and Al Hazmi moved from their apartment into a room rented to them by Abdussatter Shaikh. An Indian-born Muslim, Shaikh was a retired English professor, a leader of his local mosque—and a paid informant for the FBI's San Diego office, charged with monitoring the city's Saudi community. "He stayed at the home of a source of ours," an FBI counterterrorism official later told James Bamford, author of *A Pretext for War.*[55] "Had we known about them, we would have followed them and said, 'Hey, these guys are going to aviation school.'"[56]

The Joint Inquiry concluded that "the informant's contacts with the hijackers, had they been capitalized on, would have given the San Diego FBI field office perhaps the Intelligence Community's best chance to unravel the September 11 plot."[57] Later efforts by the Joint Inquiry to interview the informant were thwarted by the FBI and the Justice Department. (See chapter 5.)

On June 18, 2002, in testimony to the Joint Inquiry, FBI director Robert Mueller said that "while here [in America], the hijackers effectively operated without suspicion, triggering nothing that would have alerted law enforcement and doing nothing that exposed them to domestic coverage."[58] There is no way of knowing for sure whether Mueller was lying or merely ignorant. (Mueller's later efforts to cover up FBI failures are discussed in chapter 5.) But by the time it issued its report, the Joint Inquiry had found that five of the hijackers "may have had contact with a total of 14 people who had come to the FBI's attention during counterterrorism or counterintelligence investigations prior to September 11, 2001. Four of those 14 were the focus of FBI investigations during the time that the hijackers were in the United States. . . . Despite their proximity to FBI targets and at least one FBI source, the future hijackers successfully eluded FBI attention." [59]

One man who might have been capable of "connecting the dots" was John O'Neill, the FBI counterterrorism expert and the Bureau's leading expert on Al Qaeda. O'Neill had devoted years to tracking the group's activities, including trips to Saudi Arabia and Yemen after the attacks on American military targets there. O'Neill had also warned repeatedly of sleeper cells in the United States, and of the near certainty of a domestic attack. In the spring of 2001, Richard Clarke had recommended O'Neill as his replacement as counterterrorism "czar" at the NSC. But the charismatic O'Neill was considered overly independent and had also been relentless in his insistence that Saudi Arabia and its funding networks were responsible for Al Qaeda. (See chapter 5.) In July, someone at the Bureau leaked to the *New York Times* information on some careless security breaches in O'Neill's past— a leak that "seemed to be timed to destroy O'Neill's chance of being confirmed for the N.S.C. job."[60] He had made enemies, including some close to Bush. In August 2001, he left the Bureau to become director of security at the World Trade Center, where he died on 9/11.

HOW INTELLIGENCE FAILURES WERE POLITICIZED—AND REWARDED

Evidence shows that the leadership of the Intelligence Community, as well as White House officials all the way up to the president, had ample warning of the 9/11 attacks. While there is no evidence to show that they knew exactly when and where the attacks would take place, they had plenty of information about the potential nature of the attacks, more than an inkling about the targets, and a good idea that it was going to happen soon. Their inability to actually stop the attacks shows a failure of both agency performance and administration policy. Did the intelligence agencies and the Bush administration allow the attacks happen? Applying the strictest sense of the term—the meaning suggested by conspiracy theorists—no, they did not know of the hijackers' specific plans and decide not to stop them. In the broader sense, however, yes; institutional incompetence and political negligence allowed the attacks to happen.

At the CIA, Director George Tenet seemed genuinely alarmed by the threat of Bin Laden, but the agency that had been so effective at helping to create Al Qaeda proved, overall, a dismal failure at trying to bring it down. The CIA was unable to infiltrate the group and learn of the plans for the attacks, and it allowed several future hijackers to slip through its fingers—and into the United States.

At the FBI, the record is, if anything, worse. The attorney general actually told the FBI to stop bothering him with information about the threat of Al Qaeda, and the Bureau ignored warnings from rank-and-file agents like those in Phoenix and Minneapolis, and from top-ranking experts like John O'Neill. Such was the state of affairs at the Bureau that two future hijackers enjoyed the hospitality of an FBI informant while they took their flying lessons in California.

At the White House, the atmosphere of willful negligence was more powerful still. From the moment it took office, the Bush administration showed a remarkable lack of interest in any information the Intelligence Community provided about Al Qaeda, though Dick Cheney made trips to Langley to chat up the CIA leadership about Iraq. A top-level meeting on the subject, requested by Richard Clarke during Bush's first week in office, did not take place until September 4, and was sidetracked by Rumsfeld and Wolfowitz's arguments about supposed terrorist threats from Iraq. Short of a diagram of the planned attack, it seems unlikely that anything could have persuaded the White House to pay adequate attention to Al Qaeda, and provide the kind of leadership that might have prevented 9/11.

Rather than look at these simple facts—many of them documented in mainstream investigations by Congress and the 9/11 Commission—the administration and others have produced a novel piece of spin to explain away their own culpability in failing to stop the attacks.

Before the dust had settled, efforts were underway to build up the myth that U.S. intelligence had failed in the lead-up to 9/11 because the agencies' hands had been tied by crippling regulations, overzealous oversight, and inadequate funding. The real blame, it seemed, belonged not to the Intelligence Community itself, not to George Tenet or John Ashcroft or George Bush, but to Congressional liberals, peaceniks, and the American Civil Liberties Union, who back in the 1970s had conspired to destroy the capabilities of the intelligence services.

The myth, which has only gained momentum in the years since the 9/11 attacks, goes like this: In the excessively liberal post-Watergate era, when the American people were overly sensitized to covert government activities and Democrats held both the White House and Congress, two Congressional committees launched investigations into intelligence activities. These committees, as the story goes, used their investigative powers to undermine the intelligence services in order to serve their own left-leaning political aims.

In fact, the Senate's Select Committee to Study Governmental Operations with Respect to Intelligence Activities, which became known as the Church Committee, was dangerously explicit in identifying the true purpose of the FBI's domestic intelligence operations, concluding that the Bureau's actions "had no conceivable rational relationship to either national security or violent activity. The unexpressed major premise of much of COINTELPRO is that the Bureau has a role in maintaining the existing social order, and that its efforts should be aimed toward combating those who threaten that order."[61] A simultaneous—and even more contentious—investigation was carried out in the House by the Select Committee on Intelligence. The so-called *Pike Committee Report* focused on CIA covert actions and was particularly damning in its documentation of the agency's intelligence failures and out-of-control budgets.

As the legend continues, these investigations brought about a sea change in the way the intelligence agencies operated. Chastened and restrained, the CIA became soft and "risk-averse." The FBI pulled back on its domestic intelligence activities and began to focus exclusively on law enforcement. And new regulations under the Foreign Intelligence Surveillance Act (FISA), reinforced during the wimpy Clinton administration, created a "wall" between intelligence investigations of foreign threats and domestic law enforcement. This separation supposedly left the nation with no legal means of conducting domestic intelligence. (This was the legal technicality, clarified in a 1995 memo written by Jamie Gorelick, that Ashcroft claimed was "the single greatest structural cause for the September 11th problem.") All this left America with an Intelligence Community that was weakened and overly restrained, "risk averse" and broken in spirit.

As documented in the *American Prospect*, the myth making kicked in

> the day of the World Trade Center massacre on ABC, when former Secretary of State James Baker said that Church's hearings had caused us to "unilaterally disarm in terms of our intelligence capabilities." The allegation was soon repeated by Republican Senator Christopher "Kit" Bond of Missouri and numerous conservative commentators. The Wall Street Journal editorial page called the opening of Church's public hearings "the moment that our nation moved from an intelligence to anti-intelligence footing." And the spy-mongering novelist Tom Clancy attacked Church on Fox News's *O'Reilly Factor*: "The CIA was gutted by people on the political left who don't like intelligence operations," he said. "And as a result of that, as an indirect result of that, we've lost 5,000 citizens last week."62

Even George Bush *père*—who was Director of Central Intelligence when the Church and Pike reports were released—got into the act, declaring at a counterintelligence conference, "it burns me up to see the agency under fire." Recent criticism, Bush said, reminded him of the 1970s, when Congress "unleashed a bunch of untutored little jerks out there" to investigate the CIA.[63]

Some aspects of the myth were reinforced by investigative bodies, including the Joint Inquiry and the 9/11 Commission. Report after report cites the restraints placed on the FBI's methods and jurisdiction, and the resultant lack of an effective domestic intelligence operation as the preeminent shortcoming that allowed the 9/11 attacks to take place without warning. If only there had been something like COINTELPRO—or, at least, a kinder, gentler version of COINTELPRO—the Bureau might have infiltrated a U.S.-based terrorist cell and thwarted the attacks. Such ideas lead naturally to discussions of how the United States must learn to "balance" civil liberties with effective counterterrorism.

But the myth has only deflected discussions of the true problems at the intelligence agencies. In fact, the FBI has conducted domestic spying from the moment it was established, and it has never stopped doing so. No law or group of laws sets limits on what the FBI can or cannot do. The Bureau's counterintelligence activities originate from a series of vaguely worded presidential directives. And in the thirty years since the *Church* and *Pike Committee Reports*, Congress has enacted few real restrictions that would curtail such activities. David Cole and James X. Dempsey, in *Terrorism and the Constitution*, point out, "The federal criminal code includes statutes that, if interpreted broadly, would criminalize militant rhetoric against the government. Judges rarely deny requests for wiretapping. Attorney General guidelines leave the FBI wide discretion, can be easily rewritten or reinterpreted, and in any event are not enforceable in court. Guidelines on counterintelligence investigations are largely classified and are not even available for public scrutiny. Congressional oversight is inconsistent, often driven by partisan disputes rather than principle, and easily stymied by Executive Branch resistance."[64]

Likewise, the CIA has never shown signs of being seriously chastened by the exposures of its numerous covert operations, nor has it refrained from working with thugs, despite any "guidelines" to the contrary. Among other things, it provided money and arms to a budding Al Qaeda in Afghanistan, a decade after the 1970s Congressional investigations.

Since 9/11, however, the government has used the myth to provide a politically expedient excuse for the poor performance of the intelligence agencies, deflecting scrutiny from a host of politically unsavory explanations for intelligence failures. CIA oversights, FBI mismanagement, the leadership vacuum in the Bush White House—all are obscured by a chorus of right-wing finger pointing.

In fact, the Bush administration has used the myth, as part of its rhetoric of the War on Terror, to channel more and more money and power into covert intelligence operations at home and abroad. In the years since the 9/11 attacks, the CIA and FBI have enjoyed a rise in funding and an increase in their reach and jurisdiction, while pesky concerns about civil liberties and international law fall by the wayside.

The Intelligence Community's budgets for counterterrorism were already quite generous in the years between the embassy bombings of 1998 and the attacks of September 11, 2001. In the post-9/11 era, funding at all of the agencies has increased significantly. Precise budgets remain classified, but estimates place the probable total at about $40 billion, a 50 percent increase over the budgets of the late 1990s (the last years for which numbers are known).[65]

The Intelligence Community in the wake of 9/11 not only has more resources, but a far freer hand to utilize them. Congress passed the USA PATRIOT Act just forty-five days after the

September 11 attacks, with virtually no debate. The Act removes the already weak restrictions on the FBI's ability to conduct domestic spying operations, including all types of surveillance, and surrounds these operations with a far more impenetrable cloak of secrecy. By the summer of 2001, the American Civil Liberties Union found the Bureau up to its old Hoover-era tricks, spying on nonviolent activist groups; since 2001, it has compiled nearly 1,200 pages on the ACLU itself and 2,400 pages on Greenpeace, and conducted an extensive counterterrorism investigation of the antiwar group that organized the peaceful march at the 2004 Republican National Convention.[66]

At the CIA, the days of worrying about being caught in unpalatable covert actions are long over. Almost anything is permissible in the name of the War on Terror. It was CIA officials who carried out the aggressive interrogations techniques at Guantanamo, in Iraq at Abu Ghraib prison, and in Afghanistan. Press reports have brought to light the CIA's practice of "extraordinary rendition," in which, to avoid any charges of torture, the CIA sends its prisoners abroad to nations that condone torture to have them "softened up" there. Government officials who sanctioned these abuses have all gone unpunished. The nation's new attorney general, Alberto Gonzalez, wrote the initial memoranda justifying the torture while he served as Bush's White House counsel in the first administration.

The Bush administration has yet to be held accountable for its negligence, or the Intelligence Community for its stunning failures. Instead, the agencies have found their budgets increased, and their power enlarged by the USA PATRIOT Act at home, and greater support for covert actions abroad. Just as the airlines received huge financial bailouts and the FAA large budget increases, the Intelligence Community has reaped generous rewards following the attacks it failed to prevent. In the aftermath of 9/11, no failure has gone unrewarded.

4

Did U.S. "Allies" Help Make the Attacks Possible?

HOW PAKISTAN, SAUDI ARABIA, AND U.S. FOREIGN POLICY
CONTRIBUTED TO THE EVENTS OF 9/11

In August 1998, shortly after the Al Qaeda bombings of two U.S. embassies in East Africa, Osama Bin Laden was interviewed by Agence France-Press. In grandiose but concise terms, he described his own rise to power in the early 1980s, during the years of the Soviet occupation of Afghanistan. "To counter these atheist Russians, the Saudis chose me as their representative in Afghanistan," he said. "I settled in Pakistan in the Afghan border region. There I received volunteers who came from the Saudi kingdom and from all over the Arab and Muslim countries. I set up my first camp where these volunteers were trained by Pakistani and American officers. The weapons were supplied by the Americans, the money by the Saudis. I discovered that it was not enough to fight in Afghanistan, but that we had to fight on all fronts, communist or western oppression."[1]

In spite of its self-serving message and self-aggrandizing tone, the basic facts of Bin Laden's account are not inaccurate. The terrorist organization that would one day launch the most devastating attacks ever to take place on American soil owes its existence, in large part, to U.S. covert operations and U.S. allies. At its inception, Al Qaeda was trained and supported by Pakistani agents, funded by Saudi sympathizers, and supplied by the CIA.

Later, when Bin Laden turned his sights on the United States, the CIA's former friend in Afghanistan became its enemy. But the strategic and financial support provided by Pakistan and Saudi Arabia continued, right up to the moment of the 9/11 attacks. Without these two countries—and especially their powerful intelligence services—the attacks could not have taken place. Attacks of this magnitude required money, and they required a friendly regime in Afghanistan to provide a training base; these were supplied courtesy of our "allies" in the region. Their support for Al Qaeda continued over nearly two decades, with little intervention from the United States beforehand, and few consequences after the fact.

HOW THE CIA AND THE PAKISTANI SECRET SERVICE LAUNCHED AL QAEDA

After the attacks of September 11, 2001, the trail of the terrorists quickly led back to Afghanistan, where Al Qaeda maintained its camps under the protection of the Taliban regime. But in reality, the trail leads further back into Afghan history, to the final decade of the Cold War, when the Soviet Union perceived a threat on its southern border and made the disastrous decision to invade and occupy Afghanistan.

The launch of U.S. covert actions in Afghanistan was not merely a response to the Soviet invasion—it helped to provoke the invasion. In January 1998, Jimmy Carter's national security advisor, Zbigniew Brzezinski, told *Le Nouvel Observateur*, "According to the official history, CIA aid to the [anti-Soviet] Mujahaddin began during 1980, that's to say, after the Soviet army invaded Afghanistan. But the reality, kept secret until now, is completely different: On 3 July 1979 Carter signed the first directive for secret aid to the opponents of the pro-Soviet regime in Kabul. And on the same day, I wrote a note to the president in which I explained that in my opinion this aid would lead to a Soviet military intervention."

Brzezinski continued, "On the day that the Soviets officially crossed the border, I wrote to President Carter, saying, in essence: 'We now have the opportunity of giving the Soviet Union its Vietnam War.' Indeed, for almost ten years, Moscow had to carry on a war unsupportable by the government, a conflict that brought about the demoralization and finally the breakup of the Soviet empire."

Asked whether he regretted having supported an operation that fomented Islamic fundamentalism in Afghanistan, thereby giving aid to future terrorists, Brzeznninski responded, "What is more important in world history? The Taliban or the collapse of the Soviet empire? Some agitated Muslims or the liberation of Central Europe and the end of the Cold War?"[2]

The "agitated Muslims" indeed became a key part of the CIA's strategy in Afghanistan, where a full-scale covert war was carried out during the Reagan administration, with hundreds of millions in funding eventually provided by Congress. The covert operation took place under the zealous leadership of CIA Director William J. Casey, from 1982 until he became incapacitated in the autumn of 1986. Afghanistan seems to have held a special place in Casey's heart, representing an opportunity to fight the Soviets right on their own border. In his book *Ghost Wars*, Steve Coll describes Casey in his famed black C-141 Starlifter transport, streaking through the night sky from CIA headquarters in Langley to Islamabad and back, sometimes stopping off in Riyadh to drum up funding. Casey promoted the idea that would eventually blaze a trail directly from the Cold War to the attacks of 9/11. He wanted to see the formation of an "all Arab" volunteer force that could recruit Muslims from around the world to come to Afghanistan to join the jihad against the Soviet Union.[3]

Pakistan quickly became the United States' number one ally in the Afghan campaign. Although it was long viewed as a strategic ally in the Cold War, relations between Pakistan and the United States at that time had been strained by Pakistani human rights abuses and nuclear weapons development, and most U.S. aid had been cut off. According to Soviet journalist Artyom Borovik, Pakistani leader General Mohammed Zia ul-Haq "saw in the Afghan conflict a unique opportunity to obtain a sharp increase in U.S. military and financial aid to Pakistan. The Pakistani generals regarded the entrance of Soviet troops into Afghanistan as 'Brezhnev's gift.'" And indeed, soon after the Soviet invasion, Jimmy Carter described Pakistan as a "frontline state" in the Cold War, and offered Zia $400 million in military and economic aid. In 1981, Reagan increased the aid package to $3.2 billion over six years, renewed in 1986 at the level of $4 billion. This aid required waivers to Congressional measures forbidding aid to countries developing nuclear capabilities—the first of many instances where the United States would look the other way when it came to Pakistan.[5]

Zia was more than willing to support Casey's strategy of building an international Islamic force to fight in Afghanistan. According to Ahmed Rashid in his book *Taliban*, Pakistan issued standing orders to all its embassies to grant visas to anyone who wanted to come and fight with the mujaheddin against the Soviets. As a result, a growing force of Muslims from around the world gathered in camps in easternmost Afghanistan, just across the Pakistani border. These camps, Rashid notes, became "virtual universities for future Islamic radicalism."[6]

The CIA in Afghanistan worked closely with its Pakistani counterpart, the Directorate for Inter-Services Intelligence, or ISI. According to Mohammad Yousaf, the ISI operations chief for the Afghanistan campaign, most of the U.S. money and supplies were channeled right to the ISI, which then decided which commanders in Afghanistan got what weapons. The ISI maintained four base commands within Afghanistan, each of which in turn reached out to smaller units, organized around clans and villages.[7]

As reported in the *Financial Times*, the ISI even "started a special cell for the use of heroin for covert actions"—initiated, according to the article, in the early 1980s "at the insistence of the Central Intelligence Agency." This cell

> promoted the cultivation of opium and the extraction of heroin in Pakistani territory as well as in the Afghan territory under mujahideen control for being smuggled into the Soviet controlled areas in order to make the Soviet troops heroin addicts. After the withdrawal of the Soviet troops, the ISI's heroin cell started using its network of refineries and smugglers for smuggling heroin to the Western countries and using the money as a supplement to its legitimate economy. But for these heroin dollars, Pakistan's legitimate economy must have collapsed many years ago. . . . Not only the legitimate State economy, but also many senior officers of the Army and the ISI benefited from the heroin dollars.[8]

Mikhail Gorbachev made the decision to withdraw Soviet forces from Afghanistan, and the pullout took place in early 1989. By that time, reports and complaints about the growing force of militant Islamic volunteers began to come back to the CIA. But with the advent of the Soviet wind-down and withdrawal, and the subsequent collapse of the Soviet Union and demise of the Cold War, the West lost all interest in Afghanistan. The United States never made any real attempt to deal with the realities it had helped create on the ground in Afghanistan. The war left behind a country where 1.5 million citizens—10 percent of the total population—had been killed, and 6 million had fled as refugees; where a third of the towns and villages had been destroyed outright or rendered unlivable, three-quarters of the paved roads were gone, and half of the agricultural production and livestock had been lost. It also left behind a heavily armed and heavily mined country in a state of virtual anarchy.[9]

As the leaders of former mujaheddin factions fought one another for control, Afghan and Pakistani students were building a new political movement. This movement grew up around the thousands of madrassahs, or religious schools, that had taken root within Pakistan along the northwestern Afghan border. The founders of the new Taliban had no trouble finding recruits in the madrassahs and in the crowded refugee camps on the Afghan-Pakistani border, and they soon became a force to reckon with within the warring factions in Afghanistan.

Among those keeping their eye on the growing Taliban movement was the ISI, long a major instrument of Pakistani foreign policy. The jihadists within the Pakistani government, and especially within the intelligence service, were unstinting in their support of the Taliban, and the ISI as a whole looked upon the Taliban with increasing favor. The ISI would be instrumental in bringing the Taliban to power, and would continue to provide them aid and advice in managing the country once they had assumed control. At times, Afghanistan almost seemed to be an administrative appendage of Pakistan.[10]

At the same time, the cadre of militant Islamic guerrilla fighters who had converged from across the Islamic world were determined to maintain Afghanistan as a headquarters for future jihads. The time was ripe for the completion of what would prove a deadly troika joining the Pakistani secret service, the Taliban, and Al Qaeda.

HOW THE ISI SUSTAINED THE TALIBAN AND PROTECTED BIN LADEN

Like thousands of others, Osama Bin Laden had cut his jihad teeth in the anti-Soviet war in Afghanistan. Those who knew him when he first arrived, in 1980, depict him as a gentle, modest Saudi whose only desire was to put a shoulder to the wheel in ousting the Soviets. He was not considered a fighter, or much of a leader. He was considered wealthy, and over time his wealth took on mythic proportions. Although nowhere near as rich as rumor had it, Bin Laden drew on other members of the Saudi elite and helped finance hospitals, camps, and other construction projects.

Bin Laden was never viewed as a military commander until the Russians attacked his camp in eastern Afghanistan in 1987. Bin Laden appears to have been wounded in the foot (although there have also been reports of kidney problems and the need for dialysis at the time). Thanks to his own public relations campaign, he was from then on celebrated as a jihad fighter, often filmed on horseback. His experiences were told and retold in his own propaganda.[11]

As the Soviets began their pullout, Bin Laden and his closest associates "agreed that the organization successfully created for Afghanistan should not be allowed to dissolve. They established what they called a base or foundation (*al Qaeda*) as a potential general headquarters for future jihad."[12] But without a local jihad to fight, Bin Laden moved back to Saudi Arabia in 1989. Then, disgusted by the Saudi alliance with the United States in the Gulf War, he moved to Sudan, where he continued to build his operation to finance and support terrorist enterprises. He and dozens of his supporters returned to Afghanistan in 1996, just months before Kandahar finally fell to the Taliban.

Here, again, Pakistan played a decisive role. As the *9/11 Commission Report* acknowledged, "Though his destination was Afghanistan, Pakistan was the nation that held the key to his ability to use Afghanistan as a base from which to revive his ambitious enterprise for war against the United States." Pakistan would continue to be the source of madrassah-bred militants, and the country clearly hoped that the Taliban and its like "perhaps could bring order in chaotic Afghanistan and make it a cooperative ally."[13]

"It is unlikely," the Commission continues,

> that Bin Laden could have returned to Afghanistan had Pakistan disapproved. The Pakistani military and intelligence services probably had advance knowledge of his coming, and its officers may have facilitated his travel. During his entire time in Sudan, he had maintained guesthouses and training camps in Pakistan and Afghanistan. These were part of a larger network used by diverse organizations for recruiting and training fighters for Islamic insurgencies in such places as Tajikistan, Kashmir, and Chechnya. Pakistani intelligence officers reportedly introduced Bin Laden to Taliban leaders in Kandahar, their main base of power, to aid his reassertion of control over camps near Khowst, out of an apparent hope that he would now expand the camps and make them available for training Kashmiri militants [for Pakistan's ongoing standoff with India].[14]

Bin Laden himself acknowledged his debt to the ISI, which he surely must have had in mind when he told *Time* magazine, in a 1999 interview, "As for Pakistan, there are some governmental departments which, by the grace of God, respond to [the] Islamic sentiments of the masses in Pakistan. This is reflected in sympathy and cooperation. However, some other governmental departments fell into the trap of the infidels. We pray to God to return them to the right path."[15]

Cementing his relationship with the new Taliban regime (to which he brought considerable monetary support), Bin Laden helped expand the jihadist training camps in the safe sanctuary of Afghanistan; these camps would, according to U.S. intelligence estimates, train from 10,000 to 20,000 fighters between his 1996 return and September 11, 2001.[16]

In February 28, 1998, Bin Laden issued his famous fatwa. (See chapter 3.) Less than six months later, on August 7, 1998, Al Qaeda carried out its most devastating terrorist attacks up to that time on the U.S. embassies in Nairobi and Dar es Salaam, killing 224 and injuring more than 5,000. In the days following the embassy bombings, the CIA learned military and extremist groups would be gathering on August 20 at a camp near Khost in eastern Afghanistan. The reports said Bin Laden was expected. This might seem to be the moment to respond with force to the embassy attacks and kill Bin Laden. Weak as it was, at the height of the Monica Lewinsky scandal, the Clinton administration readied a response to the African embassy bombings by planning a surprise cruise-missile attack on the camp, hoping they might find Bin Laden there and kill him.[17]

But the attack was anything but a surprise. Seventy-five Tomahawk cruise missiles landed on the camp that evening—just as everyone knew they would. Twenty odd Pakistani jihad fighters died. Numerous others were wounded. Bin Laden was not there.

On August 19, the day before the planned attack, Pakistani cabinet minister Mushahid Hussain was in Saudi Arabia and on an open phone line called the head of Pakistan's Intelligence Bureau. Hussain later recounted his conversation to Steve Coll: "So I said, 'what's happening?' [He said,] 'Bin Laden is having a meeting tomorrow. He's called it a summit.' I said, 'do the Americans know?' He said, 'of course.'" Hussain concluded that "the attacks will come this evening," and commented to Coll that if he had anticipated the strikes, "Surely Bin Laden with all of his resources would have known what was coming."[18] In other words, between the Saudis and the ISI, it is likely that someone warned Bin Laden that the United States knew of the meeting and was planning an attack. Apparently, Bin Laden's "resources" included high-ranking individuals within the leadership of America's two most important regional allies.

One of these "resources" was Hamid Gul, then head of the ISI. By all appearances, Gul was dedicated to protecting the Taliban, which in turn maintained close ties with Al Qaeda. In *Against All Enemies*, former terrorism "czar" Richard Clarke writes, "I believed that if Pakistan's ISID [ISI] wanted to capture bin Laden or tell us where he was, they could have done so with little effort. They did not cooperate with us because ISID saw al Qaeda as helpful to the Taliban. They also saw al Qaeda and its affiliates as helpful in pressuring India, particularly in Kashmir. Some, like General Hamid Gul, . . . also appeared to share bin Laden's anti-Western ideology."[19]

But when the United States repeatedly asked the ISI to provide Bin Laden's location for a U.S. attack, Pakistani intelligence officers told the CIA that Al Qaeda no longer trusted them, so they could not pinpoint his whereabouts. According to Coll, "The Americans doubted this. . . . Pakistan's army and political class had calculated that the benefits they reaped from supporting Afghan-based jihadist guerrillas—including those trained and funded by Bin Laden—outstripped the costs, some of Clinton's aides concluded. As one White House official put it bluntly, 'Since just telling us to fuck off seemed to do the trick,' why should the Pakistanis change their strategy?"[20]

The CIA, in tracking Bin Laden, had desperately—and fool-ishly—turned to its old ally the ISI, which had been so useful during the Soviet occupation of Afghanistan. But the situation a decade later was quite different. The ISI had hated the Russian invaders, but many of them were more than sympathetic to the Taliban, and even to Bin Laden. Now, the United States wanted the Pakistanis to help them quell the rise of Islamic extremism, rather than encourage it. Some lip service was given to cooperation on both sides. The Pakistani government wanted to preserve a decent relationship with the United States, especially in 1998, when it was conducting tests of nuclear weapons. But it never took any real action to limit the ISI's support of the Taliban or Al Qaeda. And the ISI, always an entity unto itself, did worse than nothing. There can be little doubt that many ISI operatives were functioning, in effect, as double agents, getting information from the CIA and passing it on either directly to Bin Laden, or to the Taliban, which in turn informed Bin Laden.

ISI operatives were clearly involved in destroying enemies that threatened the Taliban. In early 1999, after Abdul Haq, the respected anti-Soviet fighter and Pashtun warlord, became an independent voice and stood up against the Taliban, the ISI called on him and told him to shut up. Haq paid them no heed. On returning home later that evening, he found his children and wife murdered. Several sources trace the attack to the ISI.[21] The ISI would subsequently be implicated in Haq's murder, as well as the murder of legendary Northern Alliance mujaheddin leader Ahmed Shah Massoud.

When General Pervez Musharaff took power in a 1999 coup, he appointed as his new ISI chief Lt. General Mahmoud Ahmed. Always a strong supporter of the Taliban, Mahmoud himself soon found new meaning in religion and started calling himself a "born-again-Muslim." By the summer of 2000, the long-standing relationship between the ISI and the CIA had "turned icy."[22]

The Agency also began to realize it could not count on the jihadists within Pakistani intelligence, and started recruiting and training its own team of Afghan assets. Whether due to divided loyalties or limited competence, these recruits seem to have provided little useful intelligence on Al Qaeda. (See chapter 3.)

WHAT THE ISI MAY HAVE KNOWN ABOUT THE COMING ATTACKS

The Taliban was largely the creation of the ISI. The Pakistani intelligence agency shepherded its rise, participated in its councils, kept away the CIA in order to protect it, and together with the Saudis appear to have warned the Taliban and Al Qaeda when an American attack was coming. It seems impossible that a major strategy debate could take place within the Taliban leadership without the ISI having some knowledge of it.

According to the *9/11 Commission Report*, based on testimony from Khalid Sheikh Mohammed and other captured operatives, just such a debate took place in the spring and summer of 2001. The Taliban's debating partner was Al Qaeda, and the subject was the wisdom of launching the planned direct attacks on the United States.

According to this account, a general warning had been issued in Al Qaeda camps in July or early August—a warning similar to the one issued before the bombing of the USS *Cole*. Bin Laden disappeared, Al Qaeda members and their families were dispersed, and security was increased. The alert was cancelled after thirty days. The Commission states, "While details of the operation were strictly compartmented, by the time of the alert, word had begun to spread that an attack against the United States was coming."[23]

As the Taliban leadership became aware of the attack plans, they initially opposed them. Their first priority was defeating the Northern Alliance, which continued to control portions of Afghanistan and to launch attacks on them. The Taliban were depending on military equipment and support from Al Qaeda. An attack on the United States might be counterproductive in that it would draw the country into an Afghan conflict on the side of the Northern Alliance.

Mullah Omar also opposed Bin Laden's plans on ideological grounds, preferring to attack Jews and not necessarily the United States. Khalid Sheikh Mohammed also subsequently claimed that Omar was under pressure from Pakistan to keep Al Qaeda operations inside Afghanistan. Matters came to a head at an Al Qaeda shura council meeting. While several top Al Qaeda leaders sided with the Taliban, Bin Laden overrode his opponents, asserting that Omar had no authority to stop jihads outside Afghanistan's borders.[24]

Given the Taliban's intimate knowledge of the plan for the 9/11 attacks—the debate within the top ranks of the Taliban and Al Qaeda, a shura council meeting, and the suggestion that Pakistan was pressuring Omar to keep Al Qaeda inside Afghanistan—it seems evident that the ISI must have known what was about to happen. In a so-called ally, this is treachery of the highest order. It is also another sad indictment of both an intelligence service that could not detect such treachery, and a White House that chose to turn its face away.

THE ISI AND AL QAEDA FUNDING

Other trails connect the ISI to Al Qaeda—and, in some cases, specifically to the 9/11 attacks—through transactions that supplied weapons and funds to the terrorists.

According to scattered news reports, Randy Glass, a man convicted of fraud who had turned informant, says he took part in an FBI sting beginning in the fall of 1998. Glass had several conversations and meetings in Florida and New York with an arms dealer named Diaa Moshen, who was trying to buy various weapons. Moshen mentioned both the Taliban and Al Qaeda as customers. At a July 1999 meeting at Manhattan's Tribeca Grill, they were joined by "businessman" Mohammed Malik and by Rajaa Gulum Abbas, who was revealed to be an ISI agent. According to Glass, in this conversation, Abbas said he wanted to buy a shipload of weapons. He also said, "Americans [are] the enemy," and "We would have no problem with blowing up the entire restaurant because it is full of Americans."

While other conversations were recorded and replayed on a segment of NBC's *Dateline*, there is no record of this conversation. In June 2001, Moshen and Malik were arrested and charged with attempting to buy stingers, nuclear weapons materials, and other weaponry. Surprisingly, they received sentences of only thirty months each. Abbas, back in Pakistan, denied trying to make any deals.[25]

This was only one of several channels maintained to provide funds and weapons to the Taliban and Al Qaeda, with apparent ISI participation and support. There is significant evidence that the ISI provided arms to the Taliban with purchases from Victor Bout, the notorious Russian arms dealer whom the United Nations has accused of providing arms to brutal regimes in Sierra Leone, Angola, and Liberia. The Center for Public Integrity, a Washington, D.C., research organization that operates a network of foreign correspondents, published a report on Bout in January 2002, citing Belgian intelligence documents it had obtained before the 9/11 attacks. These documents reportedly show that Bout earned $50 million in profits from selling weapons to the Taliban after they came to power in the late 1990s. The Center's report states, "Another European intelligence source independently verified the sales, and intelligence documents from an African country in which Bout operates—obtained by the Center—claim that Bout ran guns for the Taliban 'on behalf of the Pakistan government.' The documents do not describe the types or amounts of weapons, but said they came from Russian stocks."

There is no direct confirmation of direct ties between Al Qaeda and the Taliban in these weapons transactions, but the Taliban had, by that time, become so intertwined with the Pakistani ISI, and both of them with Bin Laden, that a connection seems more than possible. Peter Hain, the British Foreign Office minister for Europe who has led the international effort to expose criminal networks behind "conflict" diamonds and small-arms trade in Africa, told the Center's reporters that it was clear that Bout's supply of weapons to the Taliban, "and to its ally, Osama bin Laden," posed a real danger.

Another account of arms deals brokered by the ISI comes from the German magazine *Der Spiegel*, which in early January 2002 reported that Vadim Rabinovich, an Israeli citizen originally of the Ukraine, along with the former director of the Ukrainian secret service and his son, sold a consignment of 150 to 200 T-55 and T-62 tanks to the Taliban. *Der Spiegel* said the deal was conducted through the Pakistani secret service and uncovered by the Russian foreign intelligence service, SVR, in Kabul. A Western intelligence source told the Center for Public Integrity that Rabinovich's weapons had been airlifted by one of Bout's airfreight companies from his base in the United Arab Emirates.

Rabinovich denied all this, and Bout said, in a written statement, "For the record, I am not, and never have been, associated with al Qaeda, the Taliban or any of their officials, officers, or related organizations. I am not, nor are any of my organizations, associated with arms traffickers and/or trafficking or the sale of arms of kind [*sic*] anywhere in the world. I am not, nor is any member of my family, associated with any military or intelligence organizations of any country."

Bout is a native of Tajikistan and has had long-standing ties to Afghanistan; before settling in with the Taliban in 1995, he sold guns to warlords opposing the Taliban. His planes are registered to various companies, all operating out of the United Arab Emirates. In fact, the UAE has been viewed as the hub for trade to and

142 THE 5 UNANSWERED QUESTIONS ABOUT 9/11THE 5 UNANSWERED QUESTIONS ABOUT 9/11

from Afghanistan, with drugs coming out of Afghanistan on their way to the West stopping there, as well as weapons from Bout going back in. While transportation was provided by Bout's different air cargo interests, it also involved the Afghan state airlines, called Ariana Airlines.

Ariana Airlines was controlled by Al Qaeda. Al Qaeda agents masquerading as Ariana employees flew out of Afghanistan, through Sharjah, one of the Emirates, and on to points west. Afghan taxes on opium, paid in gold, also went through the Emirates and Dubai, where it was laundered into cash. Some of the money earned through this trade might well have been used to finance the hijackers. And it was even suggested that this money-laundering route captured and revived the nefarious operations of the old BCCI bank (the Bank of Credit and Commerce International). This bank had ties to Pakistan, which led it into a series of complicated and, in the end, failed attempts to control banks in the United States, before the British ultimately shut it down in 1990.[26]

Another important financier of the 9/11 attacks may have had a direct connection to the highest levels of ISI leadership. Saeed Sheikh, a British citizen of Pakistani descent, was a brilliant young student at the London School of Economics in June 1993 when he dropped out, went home to Pakistan, and began attending terrorist training camps run by the ISI and Al Qaeda. He participated in what he saw as a "holy war" in Bosnia, and then left again to fight for Indian and Kashmiri Muslims. Sheikh launched a career of sorts, capturing Western visitors to India and holding them for ransom. He was captured after kidnapping three Brits and an American, and sent to a maximum-security prison in India, where he got to know an Indian gangster named Aftab Ansari.

In December 1999, Sheikh was one of three Islamic militants released from prison in exchange for the safety of the 155 passengers on an Indian Airlines flight that had been hijacked to Afghanistan—with fuel and support from Al Qaeda. British intelligence reportedly offered him amnesty in exchange for cooperation, but he apparently refused. Yet he continued to live openly in Pakistan, and visited his family in Britain during 2000 and 2001. He picked up where he had left off, providing training and weapons to kidnappers in exchange for a percentage of the ransom they collected.

Over the years, Sheikh had been linked many times to the ISI. The London *Times* described him as "no ordinary terrorist but a man who has connections that reach high into Pakistan's military and intelligence elite and into the innermost circles of Osama Bin Laden and the al-Qaeda organization." In May 2002, the *Washington Post* reported that the ISI had paid Sheikh's legal fees during his 1994 kidnapping trial in India. Various mainstream news sources identified Sheikh as an ISI asset.

Sheikh apparently kept in touch with his old prison mate Aftab Ansari. Operating out of Dubai, Ansari played a key role in the July 2001 abduction of an Indian shoe manufacturer, who was released after reportedly paying an $830,000 ransom. Ansari was reported to have given $100,000 to Sheikh, who in turn passed it on, sometime after August 11, to Mohammad Atta.[27]

From here, the story grows murky. But an October 9, 2001, story in the *Times* of India reported that U.S. and Indian investigators had found evidence that the $100,000 transfer of funds from Saeed Sheikh to Mohammed Atta was made at the behest of the ISI. Specifically, the request had come from none other than the intelligence service's director, Mahmoud Ahmed. "Senior government sources," the story said, "have confirmed that India contributed significantly to establishing the link between the money transfer and the role played by the dismissed ISI chief. While they did not provide details, they said that Indian inputs, including Sheikh's mobile phone number, helped the FBI in tracing and establishing the link."[28]

The story of the possible link between Sheikh and Ahmed was

picked up by the world press, and seems to have received some independent corroboration from Agence France-Press, which on October 10, 2001, reported, "A highly-placed [Indian] government source told AFP that the 'damning link' between the General and the transfer of funds to Atta was part of evidence which India has officially sent to the US. 'The evidence we have supplied to the US is of a much wider range and depth than just one piece of paper linking a rogue general to some misplaced act of terrorism,' the source said."[29] To date, all primary sources for the story are from India, which has a stake in discrediting Pakistan, and few in the press have pursued it further.

In the United States, *The Wall Street Journal* was among the only news outlets to pick up the story. In subsequent months, *Journal* reporter Daniel Pearl embarked on an investigative trail that would eventually lead him back to Sheikh. Sheikh seemed to be operating as a kind of double agent, working with both the ISI and Al Qaeda. Some time between September 11, 2001, and January 2002, Sheikh met with Bin Laden in Afghanistan and then returned to Pakistan, where he apparently traveled under the protection of the ISI. That protection apparently ended when Sheikh was arrested for the murder of Daniel Pearl.

The U.S. government, along with a number of news sources, have since identified 9/11 mastermind Khalid Sheikh Mohammed as Pearl's murderer, although it has not provided the evidence to back this claim. But Saeed Sheikh was most likely involved as well. According to some accounts, the Pakistanis promised Sheikh a light sentence in exchange for a confession, and had promised the Americans that they could extradite Sheikh to the United States for trial. Instead, he was tried and sentenced to death in Pakistan.[30] It seems likely that Saeed Sheikh, a man who knew far too much, needed to be silenced lest he reveal the connections between Al Qaeda and the ISI.[31] Whether or not these connections lead to General Ahmed remains an open question.

Regardless, they are a threat to U.S.-Pakistani relations in that they stand to link the ISI not only to the 9/11 hijackers but also to the murder of an American journalist.

As for Lt. General Mahmoud Ahmed, on September 11, 2001, he was not only in Washington, but in the United States Capitol. Ahmed had spent the previous week meeting with officials in the White House, the Pentagon, and the National Security Council, as well as CIA director George Tenet. On the morning of 9/11 he was sharing breakfast with senior members of Congress's Intelligence Committees, including House Republican committee chair Porter Goss, who would later be named director of Central Intelligence, and now-retired Senate Democratic ranking member Bob Graham. Graham recalls they were discussing the mind-set of the Taliban and Al Qaeda when aids arrived to inform them of the attacks.[32]

Ahmed Mahmoud was relieved of his post as the head of the ISI three weeks later after 9/11. According to numerous press reports, he was expelled because he was considered too close to the Taliban to hold a leadership post in a Pakistan that had decided to cast its lot—publicly, at least—with the United States. The *9/11 Commission Report* contains astonishingly little information on the ISI in general, and mentions Director Mahmoud Ahmed only twice, both in the context of post-9/11 diplomacy, and Saeed Sheikh is not mentioned at all.[33] Now, more than ever, a key ally in the region, Pakistan has received large increases in U.S. aid since the attacks.

HOW SAUDI MONEY AND SAUDI SELF-INTEREST
HELPED TO CREATE AL QAEDA

The Kingdom of Saudi Arabia is the only contemporary nation-state to be created by jihad. As the Ottoman Empire began to collapse during World War I, the Arabian Peninsula was conquered with the help of the *Ikhwan* ("Brothers"), a force of crusading Muslim radicals under the leadership of Abdul Aziz, the charismatic head of the al-Saud family.

Nearly two hundred years earlier, the House of Saud had first expanded its power and territory through an alliance with the radical iman Muhammed bin Abdul Wahhab, founder of the movement known as Wahhabism, a puritanical and punitive brand of Islam. In the 1920s, Abdul Aziz sought to consolidate state power in the new Saudi kingdom by joining it to religious power, declaring Wahabbism the basis for all law and government in Saudi Arabia. It was, Steve Coll writes, "the debut of a strategy employed by the Saudi royal family throughout the twentieth century: Threatened by Islamic radicalism, they embraced it, hoping to regain control. The al-Sauds' claims to power on the Arabian peninsula were weak and grew largely from conquests made by allied jihadists. They now ruled the holiest shrines in worldwide Islam [Mecca and Medina]. There seemed to them no plausible politics but strict official religiosity."[34]

A powerful new element entered this volatile mix in the late 1930s, with the discovery of massive oil reserves in the kingdom. Two American oil companies quickly snapped up Saudi oil concessions, beating out the competing British companies. The foundation had been built for a long, lucrative—and dangerous—relationship between the United States and Saudi Arabia, in which the Americans would do almost anything to keep the oil flowing.

As early as 1943, when it authorized a wartime lend-lease aid program for the Saudis, the U.S. government declared, "the defense of Saudi Arabia is vital to the defense of the United States." Franklin Roosevelt took the time to stop off and meet with the Saudis on his way back from the famous Yalta Conference in February 1945, firmly establishing a U.S. monopoly on Saudi Arabia's immense reserves, to be exploited by the new

American-controlled oil conglomerate Aramco.[35] Everyone got rich, and the arrangement lasted until the early 1970s, when the Saudis' demand for greater participation in the exploitation of their own oil led to the creation of OPEC (Organization of Petroleum Exporting Countries) and the first world oil embargo. This move—and the American experience of the ensuing oil shortage—shifted the balance of power between the two nations, in favor of Saudi Arabia.

Like Pakistan, Saudi Arabia was also an important U.S. ally in the Cold War. The first U.S. bases were established on Saudi soil shortly after World War II, and it remained a strategic partner despite the Saudis' dislike for American support of Israel. When a Cold War battlefield appeared closer to home, in Afghanistan, the Saudis were all too happy to add their support to the covert war against the Soviets. "Dollar for dollar, Saudi aid matched the funds given to the Mujaheddin by the US. The Saudis gave nearly $4 billion in official aid between 1980 and 1990."[36] This took place under a formal agreement with the CIA, under which the Saudis sent yearly payments to their embassy in Washington, and from there to a CIA Swiss bank account.[37] In addition, unknown millions poured in from Islamic charities and other private sources.

Saudi Arabia also gave direct aid to the Pakistani ISI, and Prince Turki al-Faisal, director of the Saudi intelligence service (GID), began an active role in the Afghan operation, meeting frequently with his Pakistani counterparts, as well as with the CIA.[38]

Volunteers also poured in from Saudi Arabia to join the Afghan jihad, Osama Bin Laden among them. This exodus was one reason for the Saudis' enthusiastic support of the Afghan campaign. Its existence allowed them to kick their many obstreperous radicals into the jihad rather than cut off their heads. Providing funds, weapons, and volunteers to the Afghan war against the Soviets made everyone happy—both the Saudis' American allies, and their homegrown Muslim fundamentalists. As Ahmed Rashid points out, "None of the players reckoned on these volunteers having their own agendas, which would eventually turn their hatred against the Soviets on their own regimes and the Americans."[39]

HOW THE SAUDIS HAVE PROTECTED AND FUNDED BIN LADEN

After the Soviets withdrew and the Americans abandoned Afghanistan, the meaning of long-standing alliances changed. As with Pakistan, Saudi Arabia's support of Islamic jihadists no longer served U.S. interests. Yet it continued, and at first the United States paid it little heed.

The Saudis had long provided financial support to the madrassahs on the Afghan/Pakistani border, which gave rise to the leadership of the Taliban. Many Taliban were steeped in the religious tendencies of Deobandism, a strict school of Islam hostile to what it perceives as the corrupting moral and material influences of the West. The Deobandi creed had growing influence in Pakistan and was in tune, in many ways, with Saudi Wahabbism.[40] As the Taliban rose to power in Afghanistan in the mid-1990s, Saudi funding flowed once again. Saudi money also went directly to the Pakistani ISI, which was experiencing "lean years" after the Americans abandoned Afghanistan and cut back aid to Pakistan due to its nuclear program. And the ISI encouraged warm relations between the Saudis and the Taliban leadership, who said "they needed to learn from Saudi Arabia how to run a proper Islamic government." According to Steve Coll, "There was a naïve purity about the Taliban that attracted Saudi missionaries."[41]

By this time, Osama Bin Laden had become a growing problem for Saudi Arabia. Bin Laden had been enraged by the Saudi government's support for the Americans in the Gulf War, and by the basing of masses of U.S. troops in the kingdom. He had condemned the royal family—and many Saudis agreed with him. By the mid-1990s, Bin Laden was an internationally known terrorist and a sworn enemy of the United States. The Saudis had beheaded four of his followers for bombing a U.S. military target in Riyadh in 1995.

So when Sudan wanted to expel Bin Laden in 1996, the Saudis made it clear they did not want him back. The last thing they wanted was to have their native son "at home in detention or in jail where he might become a magnet for antiroyal dissent. . . . They were still not prepared to endure the political risks of bin Laden's trial or martyrdom."[42] They were even less willing to turn Bin Laden over to the Americans, an act that would have enraged Saudi fundamentalists.

It must have been a relief to the Saudis when Bin Laden returned to Afghanistan in 1996. Both the Taliban and the ISI worried about Bin Laden's presence, not wanting to anger their primary funding source. According to Saudi intelligence chief Prince Turki, after the Taliban took control of Kabul, they sent a message to Saudi Arabia. "'We have this fellow here. Do you want us to hand him to you, or shall we keep him here? We offered him refuge.' . . . Prince Turki recalled that they told the Taliban in reply, 'Well, if you already have offered him refuge, make sure that he does not operate against the kingdom or say anything against the kingdom.' Turki felt that the Taliban had taken charge of 'keeping his mouth shut.'"[43]

In the wake of the 1998 attacks on the U.S. embassies in Africa, the United States pressured the United Arab Emirates and Saudi Arabia to break diplomatic contact with the Taliban. In September 1998 Prince Turki flew to Kandahar to meet with Mullah Omar, apparently believing that Omar had agreed, in principle, to turn over Bin Laden. They sat down together over tea, and Turki promised financial rewards if the Taliban gave up Bin Laden. At this point, accounts of the meeting begin to diverge. In a television interview, Turki said that Omar began ranting at him, saying, "Why are you doing this? Why are you persecuting and harassing this courageous, valiant Muslim?" and, "Instead of doing this, why don't you put your hands in ours and let us go together and liberate the Arabian Peninsula from the infidel soldiers!"[44] But in an interview, Laili Helms, who unofficially handled public relations for the Taliban in the United States before 9/11, said that the two men sat down, and Turki said, "There's just one little thing. Will you kill bin Laden before you put him on the plane?" Mullah Omar called for a bucket of cold water, took off his turban, splashed water on his head, and then washed his hands before sitting back down. "You know why I asked for the cold water?" he asked Turki. "What you just said made my blood boil."[45] Bin Laden was a guest of the Afghanis, and there was no way they were going to kill him, though they might turn him over for a trial. While both are unreliable accounts from self-interested parties, it does seem unlikely that the Saudis, even at this point, would want to bring Osama Bin Laden home alive.

As Coll reports, the Americans thought that Turki's account of his split with Omar seemed "murky" and "suspicious." The Saudis had already passed on several opportunities to capture Bin Laden. And they continued to withhold information from American intelligence. The head of the CIA's Bin Laden unit—later revealed to be Michael Scheuer, author of *Imperial Hubris*—believed that the agency and the White House had become "prisoners of their alliances with Saudi Arabia and Pakistani intelligence." He argued that the CIA "needed to break out of its lazy dependence on liaisons with corrupt, Islamist-riddled intelligence services such as the ISI and the Saudi GID. . . . If it did not, he insisted, the CIA and the United States would pay a price."[46]

Above all else, the Saudis refused to take meaningful steps to shut down Saudi financing streams that led to both the Taliban and to Al Qaeda. Without financing from Saudi Arabia, there is little doubt that Al Qaeda would cease to exist.

Bob Graham, in this book *Intelligence Matter*, offers just one example of how the Saudi funding network operated. This thread in the vast network is particularly compelling because it leads directly to the two San Diego–based hijackers who slipped through the fingers of the CIA and the FBI. (See chapter 3.)

While conducting their inquiries in San Diego in early 2002, investigators for the Congressional Joint Inquiry made yet another important discovery in San Diego—a discovery that reveals a great deal not only about the source of the attacks, but also about how U.S. intelligence has supported the political priorities of the Bush administration, even at the expense of public safety.

According to Graham's *Intelligence Matters*, in January 2000, a Saudi national named Omar al-Bayoumi had traveled from his home in San Diego to Los Angeles. He made a stop at the Saudi consulate, where he met with Fahad al-Thumairy, a Saudi diplomat who was also an imam at the local mosque and known as a Wahhabi fundamentalist. Then he went to a Middle Eastern restaurant not far from Los Angeles International Airport, where, according to his account, he happened to hear Arabic being spoken at a neighboring table, and "in his typical hospitable manner invited the two young men to join him. They introduced themselves as Nawaf al-Hamzi and Khalid al-Mihdhar"—two of the future hijackers of Flight 77.[47]

It was at al-Bayoumi's suggestion, he says, that the two moved to San Diego. After staying with him briefly, they found an apartment across the street, and al-Bayoumi, in another act of purely personal generosity, paid their first two months' rent. He introduced them to the local Saudi community and invited them to his mosque. They also met Abdussattar Shaikh, the FBI informant who would soon become their new landlord. In June, the two hijackers even made a trip to Los Angeles to visit the mosque of al-Bayoumi's friend Fahad al-Thumairy, the radical imam who worked at the Saudi consulate.

Two years later, investigators for the Congressional Joint Inquiry, led by former Department of Defense inspector general Eleanor Hill, were reviewing files in the San Diego FBI office. There, they found evidence pointing to a money trail from Saudi Arabia to Omar al-Bayoumi. Al-Bayoumi was employed by a company called Ercan, which worked as a contractor for the Saudi Aviation Authority. Ercan in turn contracted with Dallah Avco Aviation, a Saudi government contractor owned by Saleh Kamel— "a wealthy Saudi who belongs to what is known as 'the Golden Chain,' which provides money to Osama bin Laden and Al-Qaeda on regular basis." This was a "ghost job" in that al-Bayoumi collected a salary of $2,800 a month plus expenses of $465, but never showed up for work. When Ercan tried to fire him, they were warned by the Saudis to keep him on the payroll or risk losing their contract. At one point, this was made clear in a letter to Ercan from the director general of Saudi Civil Aviation.[48]

In the spring of 2000, shortly after al-Bayoumi set Al Hazmi and Al Mihdhar up in San Diego, al-Bayoumi's "monthly allowance" stipend at Ercan jumped from $465 a month to $3,925. It remained at that level until the end of the year, and then dropped to $3,427, where it remained until al-Bayoumi left the United States in August 2001, a month before the attacks.[49] By all appearances, at least, al-Bayoumi seemed to be serving as conduit for money from a Saudi government contractor to Al Hazmi and Al Mihdhar.[50]

The Joint Inquiry also discovered a second money trail. In April 1998, the wife of a San Diego Saudi national named Ossama Bassnan found herself in need of a thyroid operation. Bassnan asked the Saudi embassy in Washington, D.C., to help out, and they sent him a check for $15,000. His wife then wrote directly to the ambassador's wife, Princess Haifa al-Faisal, saying she needed more and began to receive cashier's checks for $2,000 to $3,000 a month. Beginning in 2000, Bassnan's wife began signing over these checks to a woman named Manal Bajadr— the wife of Omar al-Bayoumi.

"Given that al-Bayoumi is suspected of having used these funds to support al-Hazmi and al-Mihdhdar," writes Graham, "to follow that stream of income is to trace a line from the Kingdom of Saudi Arabia to the wife of one spy, to the wife of another, and ultimately to the hands of two plotting terrorists."[51]

Details on these money trails are conspicuously absent from the final public report of the Congressional Joint Inquiry, perhaps among the extensive material that was classified and redacted. The *9/11 Commission Report* does include material on al-Bayoumi, but after considering much of the same evidence as Graham, the Commission found the evidence "inconclusive." (See chapter 5.)

Based on his investigations, Graham concludes, "On September 11, America was not attacked by a nation-state, but we . . . discovered that the attackers were actively supported by one, and that state was our supposed friend and ally Saudi Arabia."[52]

This conclusion is supported by evidence from a variety of sources. In his book *The War on Truth*, Nafiz Mosaddeq Ahmed draws together a broad pool of press accounts to document apparent funding trails to Al Qaeda from members of the Saudi royal family, as well as Saudi businessmen. One example involves a lawsuit by a group of September 11 families seeking $1 trillion in damages from Prince Sultan for helping to finance the 9/11 attacks. According to *Newsweek*, Prince Sultan's defense documents show "highly detailed new evidence of the Saudi government's role in funneling millions of dollars to a web of Islamic charities that are widely suspected by US officials of covertly financing the operations of Al Qaeda and other international terrorist groups." The money includes sixteen years of annual donations to one suspect charity, some of them for $200,000 or more.[53]

In their book *Forbidden Truth: US-Taliban Secret Oil Diplo-*

macy and the Failed Hunt for Bin Laden, French journalists Jean-Charles Brisard and Guillaume Dasquie extensively document the terrorist funding networks and their connections to the highest levels of Saudi society, including numerous front charities and Saudi-controlled banks. Their conclusion is even more blunt than Graham's: "Clearly, Saudi Arabia has played a decisive role in the spread of hard line Islam around the world, notably with the help of petrodollars, cleverly used in the framework of Islamization projects. Perfectly integrated into the capitalist system, Saudi Arabia played the market well—so well that its capital has become indispensable in keeping the world economy working smoothly. Since it had such an important energy reserve, the Saudi kingdom found its proselytizing activities protected by the world's superpower, the United States. There was no stopping the Saudis then, even though such violent groups as Hamas in Palestine, the Taliban in Afghanistan, and the GIA in Algeria depended on it."[54]

On the 9/11 attacks, *Forbidden Truth* quotes a July 2001 conversation held between Brisard, who had written a study of Saudi financial ties to Bin Laden for French intelligence, and John O'Neill, the FBI's former Al Qaeda expert who died in the World Trade Center attacks. The authors write that for O'Neill, everything began in Saudi Arabia and could be explained through this perspective. "All of the answers, all of the clues allowing us to dismantle Osama Bin Laden's organization, can be found in Saudi Arabia," he told Brisard.

O'Neill stressed "the inability of American diplomacy to get anything out of King Fahd" when it came to terrorist networks. With Bush's election, "the FBI was even more politically engaged," and that could be felt even on his own investigations of Bin Laden. "Saudi Arabia has much more pressure on us than we have toward the kingdom," he told Brisard. This, he believed, was due to U.S. dependency on Saudi oil and the State Department's need to have a "secure and stable" Saudi Arabia.[55]

Richard Clarke's account supports O'Neill's portrait of a U.S. government with limited leverage, unable—or unwilling—to push the Saudis beyond a certain point, regardless of the cost. Clarke recounts the Clinton administration's various efforts to pressure the Saudis to cooperate in tracking funding to Al Qaeda, and describes the "typical pattern of Saudi behavior" in dealing with attempted investigations as one of "achingly slow progress, broken promises, denial, and cooperation limited to specific answers to specific questions." According to Clarke, there was talk, during Clinton's last years in office, of employing tactics that had been used to disrupt money laundering by the Cali drug cartel, and even of sanctions against certain "Saudi entities." But the idea of sanctions was widely unpopular, and the new Bush administration had little interest in investigating Al Qaeda's financing network at all.[56]

Indeed, while the basic contours of the U.S.-Saudi relationship long predate the presidency of George W. Bush, the depth of the Bush family's ties to the Saudi royal family leave the United States in an even more compromised position. This relationship is well documented in Craig Unger's *House of Bush, House of Saud,* including decades of business dealings over two generations. Unger traces more than $1.4 billion in contracts and investments from the Saudi royal family to companies in which Bush family members and friends have key roles, including a bailout of Harken Energy, through which George W. Bush made his fortune. As Unger puts it, "never before has a president of the United States been tied so closely to a foreign power that harbors and supports our mortal enemies."[57]

What has been the effect of this relationship on U.S. policy and actions? Before 9/11 it must surely have contributed to the Bush administration's lack of interest in pursuing Saudi funding connections to Al Qaeda, as reported by Clarke. After 9/11, its impact is more obvious. To begin with, of course, there is the infamous airlift to safety of 142 people, most of them Saudi and some of them members of the Bin Laden family, with almost no prior questioning. This was the first of many maneuvers clearly designed to protect the Saudis and prevent a thorough investigation into Saudi connections—to the Bush family on one side, and to Al Qaeda on the other, which in some sense might have traced a line, however indirect, from the president to the terrorists. (See chapter 5.)

A week after 9/11, President Bush signed an executive order to block financing of "terrorists and their associates." Bush declared, "We will starve the terrorists of funding."[58] But just a few days later—and ten days after the attacks—confirmation hearings were held for the new U.S. ambassador to Saudi Arabia, Robert Jordan. "Tragedies of this magnitude show us who our real friends are," Jordan said. "We seek to build an international coalition against terrorism. [The Saudis] have answered that call superbly."[59] The Saudis' confidence that they are safe from U.S. scrutiny is demonstrated in their behavior since 9/11—most recently, in the famously affectionate visit of then–Crown Price (now King) Abdullah to Bush's Texas ranch in April 2005, and in their choice of a new ambassador to the United States three months later. In July 2005, Saudi Arabia announced that its new ambassador to Washington (replacing the slick Prince Bandar) would be Prince Turki al-Faisal. This is the same Prince Turki who ran Saudi intelligence for twenty-four years, and was involved up to his neck with Pakistan's ISI, the Taliban, and Al Qaeda. Richard Clarke has identified Turki as the man who "took the lead in assembling the group of volunteers" to fight the Soviets in Afghanistan, and "empowered" Osama Bin Laden to "recruit, move, train, and indoctrinate Arab volunteers" in the Afghan jihad. "Many of these volunteers," Clarke writes, "later became the Al Qaeda network of affiliated terrorist groups."[60]

The *New York Times* quoted a "U.S. official" who said of Turki,

"Yes, he knew members of Al Qaeda. Yes, he talked to the Taliban. At times he delivered messages to us and from us regarding Osama bin Laden and others. Yes, he had links that in this day and age would be considered problematic, but at the time we used those links."[61] But as the *New York Times* noted in an editorial, Turki "personally managed Riyadh's relations with Osama bin Laden," even in more recent times.[62] This "management" of Bin Laden included the decision not to arrest him even after his high-profile attacks had begun. It also included Turki's later attempts to extract Bin Laden from the Taliban—which failed, many in the CIA and elsewhere concluded, because they were meant to fail. Turki resigned from his post as director of Saudi intelligence on August 31, 2001, giving rise to theories that he knew or suspected that "something" was going to happen soon, and that it would involve Saudis, and that it would be wise to remove himself from the hot seat.

In its choice of allies, as in so much else, the White House continues to place its own political and economic agendas before the security of the American people.

5

Why Couldn't the 9/11 Commission Get to the Truth?

HOW THE REPORT PROTECTS THE SYSTEM AT THE EXPENSE OF
THE PUBLIC

Congress and the president created the National Commission on
Terrorist Attacks Upon the United States in November 2002,
with a legal mandate to "examine and report upon the facts and
circumstances relating to the terrorist attacks of September 11,
2001," and to "ascertain, evaluate and report on the evidence
developed by relevant governmental agencies regarding the facts
and circumstances surrounding the attacks." The Commission
was to "build upon the investigations of other entities," one of
which was the Joint Inquiry of House and Senate Select Committees on Intelligence, which had issued its report in 2002. Congress charged the 9/11 Commission with making "a full and
complete accounting of the circumstances surrounding the
attacks and the extent of the United States' preparedness for, and
immediate response to, the attacks."[1]

The Commission itself, in the final report published on July 22,
2004, states clearly, "Our aim has not been to assign individual
blame. Our aim has been to provide the fullest possible accounting of the events surrounding 9/11 and to identify lessons
learned. . . . what happened and why."[2]

The contradiction inherent in these stated aims becomes immediately clear: without "blame," there can be no true accountability, and without accountability, there is nothing to ensure that the "lessons" of 9/11 will be "learned."

But this is only one of many inherent contradictions that characterized the 9/11 Commission. To begin with, the Commission was created by the very institutions it was supposed to investigate, and its members were drawn from those institutions. Whether Republicans or Democrats, liberals or conservatives, these ten individuals are insiders in the dominant spheres of political and economic power in the United States, dedicated to upholding its basic power structures. Yet the commissioners took up a task that, if completed fully and honestly, would have revealed incompetence and treachery at the core—and at the top—of these very spheres of power, among those individuals and institutions whose job it was to protect the safety and security of the American people. A true "accounting of the circumstances surrounding the attacks" would illuminate deep and dangerous flaws in the ways that power is held—and used—in the United States. It is impossible to imagine this group of commissioners carrying out its task in a way that would have threatened the very structures that had spawned it.

In addition, the Commission conducted its work in the wake of a national crisis that had produced widespread insecurity. In this context, its hearings and its final report stood to have one of two effects: they could either undermine or reinforce the "system," challenge or affirm the basis of power and authority in the United States.

From the start, it should have been clear which of these two outcomes the Commission would support. While it might assiduously gather a huge body of information, and conscientiously make recommendations for future change, it would do nothing that could shake the foundations of the system. It would fall short of reaching any conclusions—or exposing any facts—that might threaten the viability of a major industry, endanger a presidency, uncover the clandestine means of reinforcing power at home and abroad, or seriously question the underlying tenets of U.S. foreign policy. Without these subversive facts, the Commission's report was destined to be incomplete. And incomplete it is. The *9/11 Commission Report* says just enough to provide ostensibly viable explanations for the devastating attacks, and supply ostensibly effective recommendations for preventing such attacks in the future. In this way, it preserves and reinforces the basic tenets of the underlying system, rather than question them. This is the unstated mandate of the 9/11 Commission, one it fulfilled all too well.

In one sense, the 9/11 Commission's work reflected what seems to have become the unofficial mind-set of the post-9/11 era. This mind-set holds that it is all right to ask questions, but asking the wrong questions—or pressing certain questions too far—can be unpatriotic and dangerous, undermining the nation at a time when we are already under attack.

By its own account, the 9/11 Commission and its 78-member staff (of whom 25 were identified as "counsel") interviewed 1,200 people and reviewed 2.5 million pages of documents. During its twelve public hearings, it took testimony from 160 witnesses. The Commission asked these witnesses many questions. But it failed to ask just as many questions and chose not to press the questions it did ask. It took a generally soft approach with a number of witnesses who bore the greatest responsibility for what happened on 9/11, including Donald Rumsfeld, John Ashcroft, and FAA administrator Jane Garvey. With others, like Condoleeza Rice, it gave the appearance of firmness, but still remained on safe ground. These high-powered witnesses may have been questioned by the Commission, but they were hardly interrogated. The Commission chose not to pursue certain potential witnesses whose testimony might have proven explosive, including representatives of our allies, Saudi Arabia and Pakistan. And it chose to take testimony from some—including whistle-blowers like former FBI translator Sibel Edmonds—in private rather than in public. Finally, it buried much of the most troubling information it uncovered in the report's 1,742 endnotes.

In the end, the Commission stayed on the safe side of a line that could not be crossed. Again, it is not necessary to search for hidden conspiracies, because the conspiracy is right in front of us and all around us; the conspirators are running the country. Those in power, in government and in business, share a tacit agreement that the system must be preserved at all costs, and institutions such as the 9/11 Commission, by their very existence, sign on to this agreement. Political power must be preserved. Economic and business interests must be protected. Allies who serve us by providing the United States with valuable resources like oil or with strategic positions in the world balance of power must be guarded. These things must be done at all costs, even if it means leaving questions unanswered about a catastrophic attack on the level of 9/11, and even if it means leaving the American people vulnerable to another such attack in the future.

When, in 1994, Congress passed a new law on air security, it spoke of creating a security system that would be "adequate to ensure the safety of passengers." As this book has shown, the agency charged with creating that system, the Federal Aviation Administration, repeatedly ignored or violated this mandate. The FAA, faced with a powerful group of airline-industry lobbyists and a revolving door between the industry and agency, repeatedly placed the interests of the industry, and its concern for the financial bottom line, before the safety of the passengers it was supposed to protect. And Congress and the White House, flush with campaign contributions from the airlines, were not likely to seriously challenge this state of affairs.

If the FAA had done its job and forced the airlines to heed numerous warnings and institute vital changes—improvements to screening procedures and reinforcement of cockpit doors, to name just two—the attacks of 9/11 might have been thwarted. Instead, on the morning of September 11, 2001, the consequences of the FAA's willful negligence would be seen with horrifying clarity.

Once the attacks—the worst incidence of air terror in the nation's history—began, the FAA was simply not a major factor. The FAA's Command Center knew that American Airlines Flight 11 had been hijacked by 8:30 that morning—before any of the other three planes had been hijacked, and before Flight 93 had even left the ground. Had it taken prompt and decisive action, one or more of the other hijackings might have been prevented, and the second World Trade Center Tower might have been more swiftly evacuated. But it neglected to follow even its own procedures, failing to notify the military or control centers until it was far too late.

The performance of the airlines, that morning, was true to form for an industry that had long been permitted to put its own interests before those of its passengers. Its flight attendants' courageous efforts to provide vital information came to nothing. Despite years of warnings, the airlines clearly had no system in place to respond to such an eventuality and did not notify the FAA, flight control centers, the military, the FBI, or even its own pilots. Tape recordings from American Airlines headquarters indicate that upon hearing of the attacks, management began discussing how to "keep this quiet" and "keep this among ourselves."

With all this in mind, why did the 9/11 Commission accept and promote the premise that the FAA and airlines could not have expected or prepared for the attacks of 9/11, and did their best to "improvise" in the face of the attacks? The Commission itself had extensive evidence to the contrary, yet it failed to hold government officials and their surrogates in the airline industry accountable.

A full and honest assessment of responsibility, with a concomitant assignment of accountability, would require the dismissal of high-level government officials. It would take to task an airline industry that now wields more power than ever through the constant threat of bankruptcy and industry collapse. It might even require an investigation into a history of negligence with possible criminal or civil liability. And it would demand genuine—and costly—changes. The 9/11 Commission did recommend a number of practical security measures, but nothing that would ensure these measures are adequately implemented. Under the new Department of Homeland Security, the airlines are far behind schedule in instituting even those improvements that are funded by the government, while other modes of transportation are sidelined under a policy of "risk assessment."

Most importantly, a full assessment would expose and disrupt the foundations of the underlying system that greases the wheels of the American political economy. It would connect, in the public mind, the emotionally charged events of 9/11 with a system where lobbyists, campaign funding, and the revolving door between government and industry conspire to place business profits before public safety, and where regulators protect the industries they are supposed to monitor, rather than the people they are supposed to serve. This is dangerous ground, ground on which the 9/11 Commission was evidently not willing to tread.

At every level, the U.S. government failed to fulfill its responsibility, spelled out in laws and regulations, to protect the public safety by reacting to warnings of a coming attack. Put in simple terms, it behaved like a cop who is told a known murderer is coming to kill you, but does nothing to protect you and does not even tell you about the danger you face. Before 9/11, the

Bush administration put the nation at risk by failing to make the threat of Al Qaeda a priority. It clearly recognized the possibility of an attack from the air using commercial aircraft in suicide raids. The famous August presidential briefing paper made the prospect of an attack immediate. But the Bush government was focused on other things, such as planning an invasion of Iraq.

Even the bare facts outlined in the *9/11 Commission Report* paint a grim portrait of government leadership during the most devastating domestic attack in the nation's history. But here again, the Commission fails to get to the bottom of the most controversial issues. And it assiduously avoids assigning accountability at the highest levels of government power—precisely where such accountability ought to rest.

The full transcripts of Rumsfeld's testimony before the 9/11 Commission shows the secretary of defense as his usual irascible self, and the Commission reluctant to take him on. Rumsfeld offers no excuses for his inaction on the day of the attacks, and even justifies this inaction with the outlandish declaration that the Pentagon had no role in defending the United States against attacks using commercial airliners within its borders; this kind of attack, he said, was a "law enforcement matter." In fact, the only real defense of America's capital city was undertaken by the Secret Service, which sent planes into the air above the city with "weapons free" orders to shoot at will. The 9/11 Commission noted this fact, but did not connect it with the utter failure in leadership by the secretary of defense.

While Rumsfeld played no role during the attacks, he moved swiftly into action when it came time to manipulate them for political gain. Late on the morning of 9/11, he was handed an intelligence memo from the NSA noting an intercept from an Al Qaeda safe house in Central Asia taking credit for the attacks. The secretary of defense had been clearly informed Al Qaeda was behind the attacks—but he was already busy writing himself notes about getting Saddam Hussein. And in a meeting of top government officials a few hours later, he was pushing for an attack on Iraq. The Commission's response to this cynical manipulation of a national tragedy, by Rumsfeld and others in the Bush administration, was to ignore it.

Rumsfeld's actions will become still more questionable if the accusations levied in August 2005 by military intelligence officers working within the Pentagon turn out to be true. Lt. Colonel Anthony Shaffer claims that the Army Intelligence and Special Operations Command in 1998 and 1999 launched a secret program called Able Danger to map out the international Al Qaeda network. According to press reports this project may have been approved by General Henry H. Shelton, then chairman of the Joint Chiefs of Staff. By September 2000, according to military intelligence officials, Able Danger had pinpointed Mohammad Atta and other hijackers working out of a "Brooklyn cell." These intelligence officers tried to tell the FBI about Atta but were blocked by Pentagon lawyers who feared controversy if the fact that the military was operating under cover within the United States— an activity banned by law—became publicly known. If Able Danger did in fact exist and if it knew about Atta, the failure to respond to this information again points to the leadership of Donald Rumsfeld, who showed no interest in the threat of Al Qaeda as he occupied himself planning for war with Iraq.

Dick Cheney was the man who gave the orders the morning of 9/11, including shoot-down orders for planes that had already crashed, and in one case for a harmless Medevac helicopter flying near the White House. The vice president has no place in the military chain of command, which is spelled out in the U.S. Constitution. Based on multiple accounts, it seems more than likely that Cheney issued these orders himself, of his own volition, rather than simply serving as a conduit for an order from Bush, as both the president and vice president have since claimed. If this is true, Cheney is guilty of violating the Constitution, and Bush and possibly others are guilty of covering up this violation.

Exposing such facts would certainly seem to be part of the job of the 9/11 Commission. But the president refused to testify before the Commission in its public hearings. Bush insisted he would speak to the Commission only in private. Even then, he would not give testimony, but engage in an informal conversation, without notes or transcript, and in the company of Cheney. A *New York Times* editorial asserted, "The White House has given no sensible reason for why Mr. Bush is unwilling to appear alone."[3] Asked at a press conference to explain the reasoning behind this odd arrangement, Bush said, "Because it's a good chance for both of us to answer questions that the 9/11 Commission is looking forward to asking us, and I'm looking forward to answering them."

In the past, U.S. presidents have testified before Congress, special commissions, or investigative bodies eight times. Ronald Reagan testified before the presidential commission investigating the Iran-Contra scandal in 1987. Bill Clinton was compelled to testify about his sex life before a federal grand jury.

But the 9/11 Commission decided not to press the issue of presidential testimony. It allowed the president to speak with them in private, without a transcript. In doing so, it deprived the public of the opportunity to see its elected leader respond to vital questions about the attacks.

More to the point, the public was prevented from even hearing the *questions* some Commissioners might have asked—questions so explosive that they were in themselves dangerous. The White House, with cooperation from the Commission, made certain that the American people would never hear anyone ask the president whether he had stood by during a time of grave national crisis, while the vice president usurped his Constitutional authority.

The questions alone, if witnessed by a broad public, might have undermined the Bush administration's campaign to use the 9/11 attacks to solidify and extend its own power. The answers, if uncovered, might have provided solid ground for impeachment of the vice president, and probably the president as well. They might have brought down a government. Here, again, was a line that the 9/11 Commission was not willing to cross.

The Intelligence Community, in many ways, took blame that rightly should have been levied against the Bush administration. In the months before the 9/11 attacks, the White House, with its sites already set on Iraq, ignored or sidelined whatever information the Intelligence Community managed to provide regarding the growing threat of Al Qaeda. But even after absorbing this misplaced blame, the intelligence agencies got off lightly in the final analysis. Poor political leadership and hidden political agendas combined with endemic incompetence and territoriality in the intelligence services. This led to an intelligence failure of massive proportions, in which both the CIA and FBI missed numerous opportunities not only to deliver detailed information about the coming attacks, but perhaps to actually thwart them.

After the attacks, the intelligence agencies applied themselves to covering up their own failures—at times, apparently, under orders from the White House—engaging in what certainly seems to qualify as an obstruction of justice.

As Bob Graham describes in his book *Intelligence Matters*, it was investigators for the Congressional Joint Inquiry who first discovered that two of the hijackers had lived in the home of a known FBI informant in San Diego. When the investigators requested all of the Bureau's files on the informant, they were summoned to meet with FBI top brass on "a very sensitive issue."

They were denied access to the informant, and when they subpoenaed him, the FBI stalled. Graham thereupon called a meeting with FBI director Mueller, along with director of Central Intelligence Tenet and Attorney General Ashcroft. They suggested that the Joint Inquiry question the informant in writing. But by the time the Bureau passed the questions on, the informant had retained a high-priced lawyer in the form of a well-known former Justice Department attorney, which Graham suspected the Bureau had gotten for him. The informant's lawyer said his client would appear if he were granted immunity. Graham writes, "It seemed strange that an individual who claimed to have done nothing wrong, who the FBI was claiming had done nothing wrong, and who the FBI argued continued to be a valuable source of information, would request immunity." The Joint Inquiry turned down the request, and it became clear they would never get to see the informant.

As Graham describes it, the FBI also "insisted that we could not, even in the most sanitized manner, tell the American people that an FBI informant had a relationship with two of the hijackers." The Bureau opposed public hearings on the subject and deleted any references to the situation from drafts of the Joint Inquiry's unclassified report. Only a year later did the Bureau allow a version of the story to appear in the public report, and even then it was heavily redacted.

Why was the FBI going through all these contortions? Graham speculated the informant might know something about the plot that would be damaging to make public. "There was another reason as well, one we wouldn't learn of until November 18, 2002, when a senior member of the FBI's congressional affairs staff sent a candid letter to Congressman Goss and me, explaining why the FBI had been so uncooperative in several instances. In discussing the case of the informant, the letter said, 'the administration would not sanction a staff interview with the source. Nor did the administration agree to allow the FBI to serve a subpoena or a notice of deposition on the source.' We were seeing in writing what we had suspected for some time: The White House was directing the cover-up."[4]

In some cases, the agencies appear to have participated in hiding or withholding information that would have exposed not only their own incompetence, but also things that the Bush administration found politically explosive.

Eleanor Hill, who headed the Joint Inquiry's staff, reported that DCI Tenet had "declined to declassify," in response to her requests, "any references to the Intelligence Community providing information to the president or White House. . . . According to the DCI, the president's knowledge of intelligence information relevant to this Inquiry remains classified even when the substance of that intelligence information has been declassified."[5]

In the wake of 9/11, a number of whistle-blowers have come forward to make public the deep and widespread problems within the intelligence services. Prominent among these is Sibel Edmonds, the young Turkish-American woman who worked as a translator for the Bureau in the fevered days following 9/11. The FBI she depicts is one where incompetence was tolerated, and even promoted and rewarded; where petty intra- and interagency competition were a fact of life; where communication was poor and paranoia rampant. She also discovered numerous security breaches and evidence strongly hinting that Islamic terrorists might well be intertwined with drug trading and money laundering, areas where the FBI and other federal agencies had set up long-standing surveillance and networks of informants. But when she raised questions about all of these things, Edmonds also discovered that the FBI was a place where a whistle-blower could be treated as a greater enemy of the state than the terrorists she had been assigned to pursue. Her exposure of what was going on resulted not in FBI investigations of the problems, but in reprisals against her, starting with the removal of her computer, having her put under surveillance, threatening her family in Turkey, demeaning her by calling her a "whore," and promising to send her to jail. The Bureau even resorted to the Hoover-era trick of attempting to portray her as a threat to national security by carrying classified documents into the Capitol.

From the beginning, Edmonds found numerous examples of inadequately skilled translators, sometimes working from lan guages they did not really speak. This resulted in the Bureau receiving incomplete or even misleading information. Then, a month after she began work, Edmonds said she was surprised when an employee showed her the file of an established Afghan FBI asset. This person was judged to be fairly reliable in that he had held a top job under the Shah of Iran keeping tabs on Afghanistan during the 1970s, and after the Iranian revolution, the FBI picked him up along with his network of correspondents. This asset had reported in April 2001 that he was receiving information that Bin Laden was planning an attack on the United States, using commercial planes as missiles. The asset's report appeared to have been taken down, translated, and filed by an agent. But then it disappeared from sight, either buried in the bureaucracy or deliberately removed and destroyed by Bureau personnel.

Edmonds did what she was supposed to do. She complained to superiors in the Bureau, then to members of Congress, then to the Justice Department's inspector general. Instead of being listened to, Edmonds was summarily fired.

Edmonds also sought to bring her information to the 9/11 Commission. At first, the Commission refused altogether to hear what she had to say. Only after members of the 9/11 families interceded with the Commission was Edmonds permitted to tell her story—to the staff, in a secure private room. The staff sat motionless, never asking a single question. When FBI director Mueller testified before the Commission, Commissioner Richard Ben-Veniste asked him in apologetic tones about the translation section. After a friendly exchange in which the two men agreed it would be best to handle this matter outside the public hearings, the matter was dropped.

Edmonds had clearly been classified as an enemy of the state. But when she refused to stop trying to tell her story and began mounting a court case to oppose her firing, the Justice Department used an arcane "security" law to try to silence her altogether. It unexpectedly invoked something called the "states secrets privilege," under which her case—articles, briefings, court filings— were classified, made secret, and removed from public discussion. Absurdly, the ruling retroactively covered the information that had already been brought to light in unclassified congressional meetings and published in the *New York Times* and elsewhere. It amounted to a sweeping gag order.[6]

The 9/11 Commission spent a good deal of its time looking at intelligence before and after the attacks. It also made a large number of recommendations for reforming U.S. intelligence in the future, most of them concerned with what it called "unity of effort" in the Intelligence Community—things like appointing a director of National Intelligence (the job now held by John Negroponte) and improving interagency information sharing. It did also suggest more congressional oversight—a nice idea, but one that is of questionable efficacy in an age when Congress marches in lockstep with the White House on matters of "national security."

What would it have meant for the 9/11 Commission to have made a full and honest assessment of the performance of the Intelligence Community, and then assigned accountability and made recommendations accordingly?

At the CIA, it might have meant abolishing—or at least rebuilding from the ground up—an agency that has proven so thoroughly incompetent at collecting and analyzing intelligence, and has carried out clandestine operations (such as the creation of Al Qaeda) that have only produced deadly blowback. It would also require an end to the secrecy that allows such covert

WHY COULDN'T THE 9/11 COMMISSION GET TO THE TRUTH?   173

operations to take place, and leaves the American people in the position of being the last to know what threatens them. At the FBI, it would have meant firing much of the top leadership and ripping apart the Bureau's legendary bureaucracy to expose its rotten core. As for the FBI's domestic intelligence operations, which suppress legitimate dissent while ignoring genuine threats, they deserve a fate worse than the CIA's.

An honest assessment would also have required the Commission to question the underlying political agendas that govern most of the work of the intelligence agencies. It would have meant assigning rightful blame to the White House, where intelligence priorities are set and intelligence information is used.

Once again, the Commission took a safer path. Their criticism of the intelligence services was extensive but restrained. Their recommendations tinker with intelligence operations rather than advocate for the overhaul they deserve, and also help guarantee that these failed agencies will only receive more money and more power in the future.

Some of the most explosive questions regarding the events of 9/11 concern the complicity of America's allies, Pakistan and Saudi Arabia, in making the attacks possible. These are also the questions most conspicuously absent from the *9/11 Commission Report*.

The Pakistani secret service, the Directorate for Inter-Services Intelligence (ISI), played an even more direct role than the CIA in creating the band of Muslim fundamentalist fighters that would become Al Qaeda. Having helped to plant the seed, the ISI also provided fertile ground. It is absolutely clear that the Taliban could never have existed without Pakistan. Much of the Taliban's leadership was nurtured in madrassahs over the Pakistani border; they rose to power with the express backing of the ISI; and they could never have ruled without Pakistan's active support. The ISI had numerous agents in Afghanistan and paid

Osama Bin Laden to train guerrillas to fight for Pakistan in Kashmir. There is evidence that Pakistan may have known in advance about the U.S. cruise missile strikes on Bin Laden's camp following the African embassy bombings, which may explain why Bin Laden himself and most of his associates had left the camp hours before the missiles landed.

While it clearly was not effective in thwarting Bin Laden's actions, the Taliban did carry on a debate with Al Qaeda over the wisdom of launching the planned 9/11 attacks on the United States. And if the Taliban knew of the coming attacks, it is unlikely that the ISI—and in turn, at least some high-level government officials—did not know as well.

In addition, there is evidence to suggest that Al Qaeda financiers—including the man who would later be arrested for the murder of Daniel Pearl—were protected, and perhaps even aided, by the ISI.

There is little doubt that some of the information the 9/11 Commission managed to gather on the Pakistani connection never made it into its final, public report, but was quashed for the sake of national security. The *9/11 Report* does document Pakistan's early involvement with Bin Laden and the creation of both Al Qaeda and the Taliban. It is less attentive to Pakistan's more recent involvement, and never seriously considers the possibility that the ISI or anyone in the Pakistani government might have known in advance about the attacks.

The United States has long viewed Pakistan as an important ally. For many years, Pakistan was seen as a counterbalance to an India that was friendly with the Soviet Union. More recently, the United States has gingerly sought to maintain its influence with both India and Pakistan, both nuclear powers who might go to war with each other over Kashmir at any moment, plunging South Asia into chaos, or worse. Over many years, the United States has poured military aid into Pakistan. These concerns would far outweigh any interest in exposing the depth of Pakistan's role in 9/11.

The *9/11 Commission Report* is even more restrained in its treatment of Saudi Arabia, the homeland of most of the hijackers and the leading financier of Al Qaeda. While it acknowledges Saudi Arabia as an important funder, it commits surprisingly little ink to its discussion of Saudi funding sources—about two pages out of 428, plus a handful of microscopic endnotes—relative to their significance in making the attacks possible. The report also signals the Commission's own position in a key paragraph: "Saudi Arabia has long been considered the primary source of al Qaeda funding, but we have found no evidence that the Saudi government as an institution or senior Saudi officials individually funded the organization." It did add, in parentheses: "(This conclusion does not exclude the likelihood that charities with significant Saudi government sponsorship diverted funds to al Qaeda.)"[7]

The report says that the Commission "found no evidence" of Saudi government involvement. It does not say how hard it looked for such evidence. Did it investigate those "charities with significant Saudi government sponsorship," to see if they might be serving as money-laundering operations for Saudi state sponsorship of terrorism in general, and the 9/11 attacks in particular? And what about the case of Omar al-Bayoumi (described in chapter 4 of this book), which the Joint Inquiry had already uncovered for them?

Al-Bayoumi is the Saudi national involved in what looked, to Graham and the Joint Inquiry staff, like a money-laundering operation, channeling funds to the same two hijackers who were living with an FBI informant. These funds appeared to come, in part, from individual members of the Saudi royal family and possibly the Saudi government itself. This evidence suggested that the Bush family's friends in Saudi Arabia were engaged in a conspiracy to finance the terrorists who would kill nearly 2,800 Americans.

Clearly, this is not evidence the White House would want to see made public. When the Joint Inquiry tried to pursue this line of investigation, it found itself once again stonewalled. The majority of its findings were classified and removed from its public report (though they were subsequently described by Bob Graham in his book).

The 9/11 Commission also investigated Omar al-Bayoumi and the Saudi connection in San Diego. They found much the same evidence as the Joint Inquiry—the same evidence of contact with the hijackers, and the same financial evidence from the Saudi contractor he worked for. But unlike Bob Graham, they found the evidence inconclusive. Relegating the information to a footnote, the *Commission Report* suggested alternative explanations for al-Bayoumi's suspicious financial records.[8] The report described al-Bayoumi as "obliging and gregarious," and stated, "Our investigators who have dealt directly with him and studied his background find him to be an unlikely candidate for clandestine involvement with Islamist extremists." (Later, when he was briefly detained in the U.K. for visa fraud, the FBI told British law enforcement to let al-Bayoumi go; he promptly returned to Saudi Arabia.[9])

Even more than Pakistan, Saudi Arabia is a nation clearly crucial to the broad political and economic interests of the United States, as a vital source of oil and as a strategic ally in the region. In addition, of course, the Bush family has long had close personal relationships with the Saudi royal family.

If the 9/11 Commission had told the whole truth and done its job, it would have held both Saudi Arabia and Pakistan accountable for enabling the 9/11 attacks to take place. It would also have looked at the changes that have supposedly taken place since the attacks with a large degree of skepticism.

Instead, the Commission had praise for Pakistan's recent "reforms" and recommended that the United States make a "long-term commitment to the future of Pakistan," urging it to "support

Pakistan's government in its struggle against extremists with a comprehensive effort that extends from military aid to support for better education."[10]

As for Saudi Arabia, a nation that should have long ago been declared a state sponsor of terrorism, the Commission argues that the Saudis are now fully engaged in fighting Al Qaeda and reports, "There are signs that the Saudi royal family is trying to build a consensus for political reform." In a recommendation that reads like it belongs in an advice column, the Commission states that, "The problems in the U.S.-Saudi relationship must be confronted, openly," so that the two countries can build "a relationship about more than oil."[11]

These two nations betrayed its ally the United States. The United States helped create the conditions for its own betrayal, let it happen, and then levied no consequences.

Oil resources and strategic overseas military positions. The nation's secret police forces, operating at home and abroad. A major industry and campaign contributor, and an underlying system of nonregulation. The president and vice president. These are some of the entities and individuals that might have been threatened had the lingering questions about 9/11 been explored with courage and integrity by the 9/11 Commission. Is it any wonder they were not?

Yet, realistic as we are about the intractable power of the "system," the idea remains that this time, things should have been different. Something as enormous as the 9/11 attacks should demand accountability from those who allowed it to happen. On the morning of September 11, thousands of Americans went to work in the World Trade Center and the Pentagon, in police stations and firehouses. Hundreds more boarded planes to begin the day's journey. Surely even the most skeptical among them must have on some level assumed that their government would protect them from attack. Surely even the most cynical among us believes that a betrayal of such magnitude must carry consequences. Without consequences, there is no justice for the dead and no safety for the living. Why has no one been held accountable? This is the last unanswered question about 9/11.

Notes

CHAPTER 1

1. James K. Glassman, "Feds, Get Off of My Cloud," *U.S. News and World Report*, 27 April 1998. For Stephen Breyer's own retrospective comments on his role in airline regulation, see the PBS series *Commanding Heights: The Battle for the World Economy*, Episode One, Chapter 14, "Deregulation Takes Off," 2003, http://www.pbs.org/wgbh/commandingheights.

2. Andrew Thomas, *Aviation Insecurity: The New Challenges of Air Travel* (Amherst, N.Y.: Prometheus Books, 2003), 43. Thomas's book is an excellent source of information and critical analysis on the history and future of airline security, and an important source for this chapter.

3. Walter Robinson and Glen Johnson, "Airlines Fought Security Changes Despite Warnings," *Boston Globe*, 20 September 2001.

4. "The Revolving Door," *Miami Herald*, 11 November 2001.

5. Doug Ireland, "I'm Linda, Fly Me," *LA Weekly*, 17 January 2003.

6. Ibid.

7. Stephanie Mencimer, "Tom Daschle's Hillary Problem," *Washington Monthly*, January/February 2002.

8. Center for Responsive Politics, "Air Transport: Long-Term Contribution Trends," Washington, D.C., May 2005; available at http://www.opensecrets.org/industries.

9. Thomas, *Aviation Insecurity*, 55.

10. *The 9/11 Commission Report: Final Report of the National Commission on Terrorist Attacks Upon the United States* (New York: Norton, 2003), 85.

11. Steve Elson, *9/11: Yes, There Is a Smoking Gun!* "Pre-9/11 Security," section 1A. This "white paper" draws on numerous unclassified internal FAA documents. Citations in this chapter are drawn from the version updated 28 September 2004. For a copy of the white paper, contact elson.atasf@verizon.net.

12. Elson, *9/11*, section 1E.

13. Don Phillips and George Lardner Jr., "Laxity by Pan Am, FAA Blamed in Jet Bombing," *Washington Post*, 16 May 1990.

14. Robinson and Johnson, "Airlines Fought Security Changes."

15. Ibid.
16. Quoted in Thomas, *Aviation Insecurity*, 53–54.
17. "Air Safety Advocate Sues Gore Over Commission Report," CNN, Miami, 8 May 1997.
18. Tom Rhodes, "Gore Sued in Row Over Report on TWA Crash," *The Times* (London), 18 June 1997.
19. See Doug Struck, et al., "Borderless Network of Terror, Bin Laden Followers Reach Across the Globe," and Steve Fainaru and James Grimaldi, "FBI Knew Terrorists Were Using Flight Schools," both published in the *Washington Post*, 23 September 2001.
20. These two whistle-blowers generously agreed to speak with the author at length and provided valuable information and perspective for this chapter. Both also supplied documents from their own files. Steve Elson, interview with the author, 22 December 2004, and subsequent e-mail correspondence; Bogdan Dzakovic, interview with the author, 12 January 2005, and subsequent e-mail correspondence.
21. Major General (retired) O. K. Steele, testimony at public hearing of the 9/11 Commission, Washington, D.C., 23 May 2003. (Full transcripts of the twelve public hearings, organized in an easily accessible format, can be found at http://www.globalsecurity.org/security/library/congress/9-11_commission.)
22. Federal Aviation Administration, Office of Intelligence, "INFORMATION: Special Analysis–Civil Aviation Incidents in the United States, 1983–1992," 16 October 1992, quoted in Elson, *9/11*, section 2A.
23. Federal Aviation Administration, Office of the Inspector General, "INFORMATION: Draft Report: OIG Survey of Airport Security," 2 April 1993, quoted in Elson, *9/11*, section 2B.
24. Thomas, *Aviation Insecurity*, 59.
25. "Official Criticizes FAA's 'Culture of Unaccountability,'" CNN, June 25, 1996.
26. "Subject: ITS Internal Communication, RE: SEA Testing," cable from Bruce Butterworth, 2 December 1997, quoted in Elson, *9/11*, section 2F.
27. "Unannounced Security Assessment, San Juan, July 16–20, 1998," after-action report produced by Team Leader Bogdan Dzakovic (initial draft), quoted in Elson, *9/11*, section 2I.
28. Memo from Special Agent Bogdan Dzakovic to FAA Administrator Jane Garvey, copied to Secretary of Transportation Rodney Slater, "Subject: Problems with FAA," 14 August 1998, quoted in Elson, *9/11*, section 2H.
29. "FAA meeting on Vulnerability Assessments for SFO airport, 9/24," quoted in Elson, *9/11*, section 2J.
30. Thomas, *Aviation Insecurity*, 85.
31. Elson, *9/11*, section 1D.
32. Thomas, *Aviation Insecurity*, 35. Also see Andrew Thomas's earlier book, *Air Rage: Crisis in the Skies* (Amherst, NY: Prometheus Books, 2001).
33. Elson, *9/11*, section 3C.

34. Federal Aviation Administration, Civil Aeromedical Institute, Human Resources Research Division, Omni International, "2001 Employee Attitude Survey, FAA CAS, March 2, 2001," quoted in Thomas, *Aviation Insecurity*, 57.

35. *9/11 Commission Report*, 4/5, n. 51.

36. Cathal L. Flynn, testimony at public hearing of the 9/11 Commission, Washington, D.C., 27 January 2004. (http://www.globalsecurity.org/security/library/congress/9-11_commission.)

37. Thomas, *Aviation Insecurity*, 59.

38. Ibid., 63–64.

39. Letter from Brian F. Sullivan to Senator John Kerry, 7 May 2001, reproduced in Thomas, *Aviation Insecurity*, appendix D, 225–26.

40. Paul Sperry, "Official: Kerry Failed to Act on Pre-9/11 Tip," WorldNetDaily.com, 19 March 2005.

41. Letter from Michael Canavan to FAA Federal Security Managers, 30 May 2001, reproduced in Thomas, *Aviation Insecurity*, appendix E, 227.

42. *9/11 Commission Report*, 18.

43. Ibid., 45.

44. Staff report, 9/11 Commission, 26 August 2004, 54. Available at http://www.gwu.edu/~nsarchiv/NSAEBB/NSAEBB148/.

45. Eric Lichtblau, "9/11 Report Cites Many Warnings About Hijackings," *New York Times*, February 10, 2005.

46. Staff report, 52.

47. Ibid., 54–55.

48. Ibid., 58.

49. Ibid., 55.

50. Ibid., 57.

51. Lichtblau, "9/11 Report Cites Many Warnings."

52. Robert Cohen, "Newark Airport got warnings before 9/11: A new Kean commission report surfaces," *Newark Star-Ledger*, 11 February 2005.

53. *9/11 Commission Report*, 14–18.

54. Ibid., 453, n. 31.

55. Ibid., 4.

56. Paul Thompson and the Center for Cooperative Research, *The Terror Timeline: A Comprehensive Chronicle of the Road to 9/11—and America's Response* (New York: HarperCollins, 2004), 357–58.

57. Recording played at public hearing of the 9/11 Commission, Washington, D.C., January 27, 2004. (http://www.globalsecurity.org/security/library/congress/9-11_commission.)

58. David Johnston and Jim Dwyer, "Pre-9/11 Files Show Warnings Were More Dire and Persistent," *New York Times*, 18 April 2004.

59. Staff statement no. 17, 9/11 Commission, quoted in Thompson, *The Terror Timeline*, 370.

60. *9/11 Commission Report*, 6, 453, n. 32.

61. Gail Sheehy, "Stewardesses ID'd Hijackers Early, Transcripts Show," *New York Observer*, 11 February 2004.

62. Eric Lichtblau, "After the Attack: A Desperate Flight," *Los Angeles Times*, 20 September 2001.

63. Gail Sheehy, "9/11 Tapes Reveal Ground Personnel Muffled Attacks," *New York Observer*, 17 June 2004.

64. *9/11 Commission Report*, 6–7.

65. Sheehy, "9/11 Tapes Reveal Ground Personnel Muffled Attacks." Also see Gerald R. Arpey, testimony at a public hearing of the 9/11 Commission, Washington, D.C., 27 January 2005. (http://www.globalsecurity.org/security/library/congress/9-11_commission.)

66. *9/11 Commission Report*, 5.

67. Ibid., 18–20.

68. United Press International, "Insider Notes," 6 March 2002. The UPI story cited a 17 September 2001 report in the Israeli newpaper *Ha'aretz*, which identified passenger and Boston resident Daniel Lewin as "a former member of the Israel Defense Force Sayaret Matkal, a top-secret counter-terrorist unit, whose Unit 269 specializes in couter-terrorism activities outside Israel."

69. *9/11 Commission Report*, 21–22.

70. Scott McCartney and Susan Carey, "American, United Watched and Worked in Horror as Sept. 11 Hijackings Unfolded," *Wall Street Journal*, 15 October 2001.

71. Corky Siemaszko, "Passengers Battled WTC Hijack," *Daily News*, New York, 9 March 2004.

72. *9/11 Commission Report*, 22–23.

73. Ibid., 287–289.

74. McCartney and Carey, "American, United Watched and Worked in Horror."

75. Ibid.

76. *9/11 Commission Report*, 25.

77. Ibid., 26–27.

78. Ibid., 10.

79. Ibid., 10–11.

80. Ibid., 11.

81. Ibid., 13.

82. Ibid., 29.

83. Ibid., 30.

84. Thomas, *Aviation Insecurity*, 68–71.

85. Ibid., 71–72.

86. Ibid., 73.

87. Ireland, "I'm Linda, Fly Me."

88. Thomas, *Aviation Insecurity*, 73.

89. Ibid., 73.

90. Ireland, "I'm Linda, Fly Me."

91. BBC Business News, "Aviation Jobs Losses Reach 400,000," http://www.news.bbc.co.uk/hi/english/business, 11 January 2002.
92. Thomas, *Aviation Insecurity*, 88–89.
93. Ibid., 118.
94. House of Representatives, Committee on Homeland Security, Democratic Office, "Department of Homeland Security: Missed Deadlines—Missed Opportunities to Secure America," 15 July 2005, http://www.hsc-democrats.house.gov/HS/Investigations+and+Report.
95. Blake Morrison Alan Levin, "FAA Security Chief Quits Over Assignment," *USA Today*, 11 October 2001.
96. "UAL Gives New CEO $3 Million Signing Bonus, Stock," Associated Press, 28 October 2002.
97. James F. Peltz, "A Tenacious CEO Keeps United Flying," *Los Angeles Times*, 24 July 2005.
98. "Tilton: UAL CEO Gets Bonus as Employees Face Cuts," Faces of the Week, 14-18 March 2005, Forbes.com.
99. Greg Levine, "AMR CEO Refuses Pay Raise," Forbes.com, 29 July 2004.
100. Eric Lipton, "Report Presses Easy Ways to Fix Airline Security," *New York Times*, 5 June 2005.
101. Gary Stoller, "Airliners May Get Missile Defenses," *USA Today*, 13 July 2005.
102. Center for Responsive Politics, "Defense: Top Contributors to Federal Candidates and Parties," Washington, D.C., May 2005; available at http://www.opensecrets.org/industries.
103. Elson, interview with the author.

CHAPTER 2

1. William Langley, "Revealed: What Really Went on During Bush's 'Missing Hours,'" *Daily Telegraph* (U.K.), 16 December 2001.
2. Scot J. Paltrow, "Government Accounts of 9/11 Reveal Gaps and Inconsistencies," *Wall Street Journal* online, 23 March 2004, http://wsj.com.
3. "Remarks by President Bush at Emma Booker Elementary School, Sarasota Florida," Federal News Service, 11 September 2001, http://www.fnsg.com/archive/htm.
4. Scot J. Paltrow, "Government Accounts of 9/11 Reveal Gaps and Inconsistencies." *The 9/11 Commission Report: Final Report of the National Commission on Terrorist Attacks Upon the United States* (New York: Norton, 2003), 32–33.
5. *9/11 Commission Report*, 39.
6. Multiple examples of perceived threats to Bush on 9/11 are documented in Paul Thompson and the Center for Cooperative Research, *The Terror Timeline: A Comprehensive Chronicle of the Road to 9/11—and America's Response* (New York: HarperCollins, 2004), 418–19, 457, 460. Thompson's timeline is

184   NOTES TO CHAPTER 2

an invaluable source for tracking the movements of Bush, Cheney, and others
on the day of the attacks.

7. James Bamford, *A Pretext for War: 9/11, Iraq, and the Abuse of America's Intel-
    ligence Agencies* (New York: Doubleday, 2004), 86; Thompson, *The Terror
    Timeline*, 460–61.
8. *9/11 Commission Report*, 40.
9. Thompson, *The Terror Timeline*, 462–63; Scot J. Paltrow, "Government
    Accounts of 9/11 Reveal Gaps and Inconsistencies."
10. William Safire, "Inside the Bunker," *New York Times*, 13 September 2001; Mike
    Allen, "White House Drops Claim of Threat to Bush," *Washington Post*, 27
    September 2001.
11. Richard Clarke, *Against All Enemies: Inside America's War on Terror* (New York:
    Simon & Schuster, 2004), 23–24.
12. *9/11 Commission Report*, 40. Some accounts, including Richard Clarke's, have
    Cheney arriving in the bunker as much as half an hour earlier, before the Pen-
    tagon crash. See Thompson, *The Terror Timeline*, 426.
13. Dan Balz and Bob Woodward, "America's Chaotic Road to War," *Washington
    Post*, 27 January 2002; and Alan Levin, Marilyn Adams, and Blake Morrison,
    "Terror Attacks Brought Drastic Decision: Clear the Skies," *USA Today*, 12
    September 2001.
14. *9/11 Commission Report*, 36.
15. Richard Clarke, *Against All Enemies*, 18.
16. *9/11 Commission Report*, 16–17, 37.
17. Ibid., 40.
18. Ibid., 40.
19. Ibid., 40.
20. Dan Balz and Bob Woodward, "America's Chaotic Road to War."
21. *9/11 Commission Report*, 41; Daniel Klaidman and Michael Hirsch, "Who was
    Really in Charge?," *Newsweek*, 28 June 2004.
22. *9/11 Commission Report*, 41.
23. Ibid., 91–92.
24. Ibid., 42.
25. Donald Rumsfeld, testimony at a public hearing of the 9/11 Commission,
    Washington, D.C., 23 March 2004. (http://www.globalsecurity.org/
    security/library/congress/9-11_commission.)
26. Donald Rumsfeld, "Secretary Rumsfeld Interview for Parade Magazine" (with
    Lyric Wallwork Winik), News Transcripts, Department of Defense, Washing-
    ton, D.C., 12 October 2001, http://www.defenselink.mil/transcripts/2001.
27. Ibid.
28. *9/11 Commission Report*, 44.
29. William B. Scott, "Exercise Jump-Starts Response to Attacks," *Aviation Week
    and Space Technology*, 3 June 2002.
30. *9/11 Commission Report*, 43.

31. Ibid., 37.
32. Department of Defense, Transcript of Air Threat Conference Call, 11 September 2001, quoted in the *9/11 Commission Report*, 43.
33. Rumsfeld, 9/11 Commission testimony.
34. Ibid.
35. Ibid.
36. CBS News, "Plans for Iraq Attack Began on 9/11," 4 September 2002.
37. Clarke, *Against All Enemies*, 30.
38. Ibid., 41–43.
39. Ibid., 30–31.
40. *9/11 Commission Report*, 16–17.
41. Ibid., 43.
42. Ibid., 43.
43. Ibid., 44.
44. Ibid., 45.
45. Ibid., 45.

CHAPTER 3

1. See details later in this chapter, and see Bob Graham with Jeff Nussbaum, *Intelligence Matters: The CIA, the FBI, Saudi Arabia, and the Failure of America's War on Terror* (New York: Random House, 2004), 11–13, 18–21, and 24–26.
2. Statistics and mission statements in the preceding paragraphs are from http://www.cia.gov and http://www.fbi.gov.
3. Senate Select Committee on Intelligence and House Permanent Select Committee on Intelligence, *Joint Inquiry into Intelligence Activities Before and After the Attacks of September 11, 2001*, 107th Cong., 2d sess., February 2002, S. Rep. 107-35, H. Rep. 107-792, 107th Cong., 2d sess.), 4. Available at http://www.gpoaccess.gov/serialset/creports/911.
4. Chalmers Johnson, "Improve the CIA? Better to Abolish It," *San Francisco Chronicle*, 22 February 2004.
5. See Chalmers Johnson, *Blowback: The Costs and Consequences of American Empire*, 2nd ed. (New York: Owl Books, 2004).
6. Graham, *Intelligence Matters*, 69.
7. Senate and House Select Committees, *Joint Inquiry Report*, 4.
8. Ibid., 91.
9. James Bamford, *A Pretext for War: 9/11, Iraq, and the Abuse of America's Intelligence Agencies* (New York: Doubleday, 2004), 235.
10. Senate and House Select Committees, *Joint Inquiry Report*, 90.
11. Ibid., 110–11.
12. Ahmed Rashid, *Taliban: Militant Islam, Oil, and Fundamentalism in Central Asia* (New Haven: Yale University Press, 2000), 134.

13. Chalmers Johnson, review of *Ghost Wars: The Secret History of the CIA, Afghanistan and bin Laden*, by Steve Coll, *London Review of Books*, 21 October 2004.

14. Senate and House Select Committees, *Joint Inquiry Report*, 104.

15. Richard Clarke, *Against All Enemies: Inside America's War on Terror* (New York: Simon & Schuster, 2004), 204.

16. Clarke, *Against All Enemies*, 223.

17. The so-called Pike Report was classified and suppressed. A version was leaked to the *Village Voice* and subsequently published in book form in the UK. See *Village Voice*, 16 February 1976 and *The Pike Report* (Nottingham, England: Spokesman Books, 1977).

18. Richard Clarke, "Presidential Policy Initiative/Review—The *Al-Qida* Network," memo to Condoleeza Rice, 25 January 2001. Transcripts of the memo and attached reports can be found at http://www.truthout.org/cgi-bin/artman/exec/view.cgi/37/8951.

19. Cited in Graham, *Intelligence Matters*, 106.

20. Ibid., 112.

21. Senate and House Select Committees, *Joint Inquiry Report*, 7–8.

22. Ibid., 7.

23. Ibid., 9.

24. "Bin Laden Determined to Strike in U.S.," Presidential Daily Briefing, 6 August 2001, declassified and approved for release 10 April 2004. A copy of the memo can be found at http://www.news.findlaw.com/hdocs/docs/terrorism/80601pdb.

25. Senate and House Select Committees, *Joint Inquiry Report*, 9.

26. Graham, *Intelligence Matters*, 173.

27. For news accounts on terrorists plans to use planes as weapons against the United States, see: "Bush: Memo Had 'No Actionable Intelligence,'" CNN.com, 12 April 2004, http://www.cnn.com/2004/ALLPOLITICS/04/11/911.investigation/index.html.

28. David E. Sanger, "Leaders Tell of Plot to Kill Bush in Genoa," *New York Times*, 26 September 2001; "Genoa Set for Summit Onslaught," BBC News, 18 July 2001.

29. Senate and House Select Committees, *Joint Inquiry Report*, 42.

30. Clarke, *Against All Enemies*, 227–28.

31. *9/11 Commission Report*, 204.

32. Clarke, *Against All Enemies*, 231–32, 237.

33. CNN.com, April 12, 2004. These and other warnings, as reported in the international press, have been compiled by Paul Thompson in his *Complete 911 Timeline*; see http://www.cooperativeresearch.org/timeline.jsp?timeline=complete_911_timeline&before_9/11=foreignIntelligence. Sources for warnings cited in this book are as follows: Nicholas Rufford, "MI 6 Warned US of Al-Qaeda Attacks," *The Sunday Times* (London), 9 June 2002; Michael Evans, "Spy Chiefs Warned Ministers of Al Qaeda Attacks," *The Times* (London), 14 June 2002; Torcuil Crichton, "Britain Warned US to Expect September 11

al-Qaeda Hijackings," *Sunday Herald* (London), 19 May 2002; "Experts Talk About Failure of Secret Service," *Frankfurter Allgemeine Zeitung*, 13 September 2001; Jim Stewart, "Sept. 11 Hijackers Made Test Flights," "CBS Evening News," 9 October 2002; John K. Cooley, "Other Unheeded Warnings Before 9/11?" *International Herald Tribune*, 21 May 2002; Carl Cameron, "Clues Alerted White House to Potential Attacks," foxnews.com, 17 May 2002, http://www.foxnews.com/story/0,2933,53065,00.html; "Russia Gave Clear Warning," Agence France-Presse, 16 September 2001; "Days Before, Priest Predicted Plane Attacks on U.S.," zenit.org, 16 September 2001, http://zenit.org/english/visualizza.phtml?sid=9943; Sebastian Rotella and Josh Meyer, "Wiretaps May Have Foretold Terror Attacks," *Los Angeles Times*, 29 May 2002.

34. Graham, *Intelligence Matters*, 113.
35. Ibid., 84.
36. Dan Eggen and Walter Pincus, "Ashcroft's Efforts on Terrorism Criticized: Ex-FBI Official Doubted Priorities," *Washington Post*, 14 April 2004.
37. Philip Shenon and Lowell Bergman, "9/11 Panel Is Said to Offer Harsh Review of Ashcroft," *New York Times*, 13 April 2004. Also see Center for American Progress, "Terrorism Not a Priority for Ashcroft Pre-9/11," http://www.americanprogress.org, 13 April 2004.
38. Senate Select Committee (Church Committee), *Final Report of the Select Committee to Study Governmental Operations with Respect to Intelligence Activities, Intelligence Activities and the Rights of Americans*, 94th Cong., 2nd sess., April 1976, S. Rep. 94-755, introduction and summary. Available at http://www.aarclibrary.org/publib/church/reports/book2/contents.htm.
39. David Cole and James X. Dempsey, *Terrorism and the Constitution: Sacrificing Civil Liberties in the Name of National Security* (New York: New Press, 2002), 21–60.
40. See Frank Donner, introduction to *The Age of Surveillance: The Aims & Methods of America's Political Intelligence System* (New York: Knopf, 1980).
41. See James Ridgeway, introduction to *Blood in the Face: The Ku Klux Klan, Aryan Nations, Nazi Skinheads, and the Rise of a New White Culture*, (New York: Thunder's Mouth Press, 1995).
42. Senate and House Select Committees, *Joint Inquiry Report*, 4–5.
43. Ibid., 48.
44. Ibid., 38.
45. Ibid., 56.
46. Ibid., 70.
47. Sibel Edmonds, interviews by the author, December 2004–June 2005. Also see Edmonds's web site, http://www.justacitizen.com.
48. Senate and House Select Committees, *Joint Inquiry Report*, 59–61.
49. Ibid., 30-31.
50. Ibid., 22.

51. Ibid., 23–24.
52. Ibid., 12–16. The story of these two hijackers—and of uncovering the information about them—also appears in Graham's *Intelligence Matters.*
53. Ibid., 86.
54. Ibid., 15.
55. See Graham, *Intelligence Matters,* 11–13, 18–21, and 24–26.
56. Bamford, *A Pretext for War,* 231.
57. Senate and House Select Committees, *Joint Inquiry Report,* 19.
58. Robert Mueller, testimony to Joint Inquiry, quoted in Graham, *Intelligence Matters,* 137.
59. Senate and House Select Committees, *Joint Inquiry Report,* 27.
60. Lawrence Wright, "The Counter-terrorist," *New Yorker,* 14 January 2002.
61. Senate Select Committee, *Church Committee Report,* introduction.
62. Chris Mooney, "Back to Church," *American Prospect Online,* 5 November 2001, http://www.prospect.org/web/page.ww?section=root&name=ViewPrint&articleId=5963.
63. Bob Drogin, "Spy Agencies Fear Some Applicants Are Terrorists," *LA Times,* March 8, 2005.
64. Cole and Dempsey, *Terrorism and the Constitution,* 67.
65. Douglas Jahl, "Disclosing Intelligence Budgets Might Be Easiest of 9/11 Panel's Recommendations," *New York Times,* 29 July 2004.
66. See http://www.aclu.org/spyfiles.

CHAPTER 4

1. "Laden Planned a Global Islamic Revolution in 1995," Agence France-Press, 27 August 1998.
2. "Interview with Zbigniew Brzezinski," *Le Nouvel Observateur* (Paris), 15–21 January 1998. Excerpt in English translation available at http://www.globalresearch.ca/articles/BRZ110A.html.
3. Steve Coll, *Ghost Wars: The Secret History of the CIA, Afghanistan, and Bin Laden, from the Soviet Invasion to September 10, 2001* (New York: Penguin, 2004), 89–106.
4. Artyom Borovik, *The Hidden War: A Russian Journalist's Account of the Soviet War in Afghanistan* (New York: Grove Press, 1990), 11.
5. Federal Research Division, U.S. Library of Congress, *Pakistan,* Country Studies Handbook Series (Washington, D.C.: U.S. Government Printing Office, 1998), "The ZiaRegime," http://www.countrystudies.us/pakistan/22.htm.
6. Ahmed Rashid, *Taliban: Militant Islam, Oil, and Fundamentalism in Central Asia* (New Haven: Yale University Press, 2000), 130.
7. Mohammad Yousaf and Mark Adkin, *Afghanistan—The Bear Trap: The Defeat of a Superpower* (Havertown, Pa.: Casemate, 1992), 117.

8. B. Raman, "Heroin, Taliban and Pakistan," *The Financial Times* (Asian edition), 10 August 2001.

9. "Backgrounder on Afghanistan: History of the War," Human Rights Watch, October 2001, www.hrw.org/backgrounder/asia/afghan-bck1023.htm.

10. Rashid, *Taliban*, 17–30.

11. Coll, *Ghost Wars*, 162–64.

12. *The 9/11 Commission Report: Final Report of the National Commission on Terrorist Attacks Upon the United States* (New York: Norton, 2003), 56.

13. Ibid., 63–64.

14. Ibid., 64–65.

15. "Interview with Osama Bin Laden," *Time*, 11 January 1999.

16. *9/11 Commission Report*, 470, n. 78.

17. Coll, *Ghost Wars*, 409–10.

18. Ibid., 410.

19. Richard Clarke, *Against All Enemies: Inside America's War on Terror* (New York: Simon & Schuster, 2004), 189.

20. Coll, *Ghost Wars*, 445.

21. Ibid., 444.

22. Ibid., 515–16.

23. *9/11 Commission Report*, 250–51.

24. *9/11 Commission Report*, 251–52.

25. Chris Hansen and Ann Curry, "Trail of Terror," NBC's *Dateline*, 2 August 2002.

26. Phillip van Niekerk and André Verlöy, "Africa's 'Merchant of Death' Sold Arms to the Taliban," Center for Public Integrity, Washington, D.C., 31 January 2002, http://www.publicintegrity.org/report.aspx?aid=245.

27. Paul Thompson, "Sept. 11's Smoking Gun: The Many Faces of Saeed Sheikh," 2002, updated 2005, www.cooperativeresearch.org/essay.jsp?article=essaysaeed. Additional sources cited by Thompson include Maria Ressa, "Bin Laden's Finger on Kashmir Trigger," CNN.com, 12 June 2002; "Profile: Omar Saeed Sheikh," BBC News, 16 July 2002; and Robert Sam Anson, "The Journalist and the Terrorist," *Vanity Fair*, August 2002.

28. Manoj Joshi, "India Helped FBI Trace ISI-Terrorist Links," *Times* (India), 9 October 2001.

29. "India Accuses Ex Pakistan Spy Chief of Links to US Attacker: Report," Agence France-Presse, 10 October 2001.

30. See Daniel Klaidman, "Federal Grand Jury Set to Indict Sheikh," *Newsweek* online, 13 March 2002, http://www.msnbc.com/news/723527.asp.

31. See Thompson, "Sept. 11's Smoking Gun," and "U.S. Officials Say 9/11 Mastermind Killed Pearl," CNN.com, 21 October 2003, http://www.cnn.com/2003/US/10/21/pearl.mohammed/index.html.

32. Bob Graham with Jeff Nussbaum, *Intelligence Matters: The CIA, the FBI, Saudi Arabia, and the Failure of America's War on Terror* (New York: Random House, 2004), ix–xi.

33. Thompson, "Sept. 11's Smoking Gun."
34. Coll, *Ghost Wars*, 75–77.
35. Anthony Sampson, *The Seven Sisters: The Great Oil Companies and the World They Shaped* (New York: Bantam, 1979).
36. Rashid, *Taliban*, 197.
37. Coll, *Ghost Wars*, 82.
38. Ibid., 78.
39. Rashid, *Taliban*, 129.
40. Ibid., 88-90.
41. Coll, *Ghost Wars*, 295–97.
42. Ibid., 341–42
43. Ibid., 341–42.
44. ABC's *Nightline*, 10 December 2001, as quoted in Coll, *Ghost Wars*, 414.
45. Camelia Ford and James Ridgeway, "The Accidental Operatives," *Village Voice*, 6 June 2001.
46. Coll, *Ghost Wars*, 415. For Scheuer's own account, see Michael Sheuer, *Imperial Hubris: Why the West Is Losing the War on Terror* (Washington, D. C., Potomac Books, 2004).
47. Graham, *Intelligence Matters*, 11–12.
48. Ibid., 167.
49. *9/11 Commission Report*, 515, n. 18. The Commission's data is based upon Saudi Civil Aviation employment records, provided to the Commission by the FBI.
50. Graham, *Intelligence Matters*, 167.
51. Ibid., 168.
52. Ibid., 169.
53. Michael Isikoff and Mark Hosenball, "A Legal Counterattack," *Newsweek*, April 16, 2003, quoted in Nafiz Mosaddeq Ahmed, *The War on Truth: 9/11, Disinformation, and the Anatomy of Terrorism* (Northampton, Mass.: Interlink, 2005), 124. For other examples, see the rest of chapter 5 in Ahmed's book (119–133).
54. Jean-Charles Brisard and Guillaume Dasquie, *Forbidden Truth: US-Taliban Secret Oil Diplomacy and the Failed Hunt for Bin Laden* (New York: Thunder's Mouth Press/Nation Books, 2002), 82.
55. Ibid., xxix.
56. Clarke, *Against All Enemies*, 191–196.
57. Craig Unger, "How Does the Saudi relationship with the Bush Family Affect U.S. Foreign Policy?," *Slate*, 6 July 2004, http://www.slate.msn.com/id/2103239/ entry/2103433/. Also see Craig Unger, *House of Bush, House of Saud: The Secret Relationship Between the World's Two Most Powerful Dynasties* (New York: Scribner, 2003).
58. Senate Select Committee on Intelligence and House Permanent Select Committee on Intelligence, *Joint Inquiry into Intelligence Activities Before and After*

the Attacks of September 11, 2001, 107th Cong., 2d sess., February 2002, S. Rep. 107-35, H. Rep. 107-792, 116.

59. Unger, "How Does the Saudi relationship with the Bush Family Affect U.S. Foreign Policy?"

60. Clarke, *Against All Enemies,* 52.

61. Steven R. Weissman, "Saudi Arabia's Longtime Ambassador to the U.S. Is Resigning," *New York Times,* 21 July 2005.

62. "Prince Turki's Résumé," editorial, *New York Times,* 31 July 2005.

CHAPTER 5

1. Intelligence Authorization Act for Fiscal Year 2003, Public Law 107-306, 107th Cong., 2d sess., (November 27, 2002).

2. *The 9/11 Commission Report: Final Report of the National Commission on Terrorist Attacks Upon the United States* (New York: Norton, 2003), xvi–xvii.

3. "The President's Testimony," editorial, *New York Times,* 29 April 2004.

4. Bob Graham with Jeff Nussbaum, *Intelligence Matters: The CIA, the FBI, Saudi Arabia, and the Failure of America's War on Terror* (New York: Random House, 2004), 160–66.

5. Eleanor Hill, *Staff Statement,* given at the public hearing of the Joint House/Senate Intelligence Committee, Washington, D.C., 18 September, 2002. Complete transcripts of the nine public hearings conducted by the Joint Inquiry are available at http://www.fas.org/irp/congress/2002-hr/index.html.

6. Sibel Edmonds, interviews by the author, December 2004–June 2005. Also see Edmonds's web site, http://www.justacitizen.com.

7. *9/11 Commission Report,* 171.

8. Ibid., 515, n. 18.

9. *9/11 Commission Report,* 218.

10. Ibid., 367–69.

11. Ibid., 374.

ABOUT THE AUTHOR

Currently the Washington correspondent for the *Village Voice*, James Ridgeway has also written for *Harper's*, *The Economist*, *The New York Times Magazine*, *The Nation*, *The New Republic*, *Parade*, *Ramparts*, and *The Wall Street Journal*; authored over fifteen books; and co-directed the films *Blood in the Face* and *Feed*.